W0115663

GETTING THERE

Successful 007 Investing for Anyone

STANLEY SMITH

Individual economic empowerment to effect lasting social change

© Stanley Smith 2021

ISBN: 978-1-09835-824-2

eBook ISBN: 978-1-09835-825-9

All rights reserved. This book or any portion thereof may not be reproduced or used in any manner whatsoever without the express written permission of the publisher except for the use of brief quotations in a book review.

*Individual economic empowerment to
effect lasting social change*

© Stanley Smith 2021

ISBN: 978-1-09835-824-2

eBook ISBN: 978-1-09835-825-9

All rights reserved. This book or any portion thereof may not be reproduced or used in any manner whatsoever without the express written permission of the publisher except for the use of brief quotations in a book review.

For my mother Ellouise and father Elijah, who gave me the morals, values, and work ethic I have today. For my extended family and friends and for my wonderful wife, daughters, and son.

FOREWORD

I must tell you that I was always working to get there to be professionally and financially successful. I'm sure you are too. My efforts included working multiple jobs such as; on a paper route, at a bakery, department store, and grocery store. I tried to start many businesses, some with partners and some by myself. At the time, I didn't know that my drive was about getting there. My drive was connected to the notion that I didn't want to depend on others for my future.

Admittedly, I wasn't successful in many cases, but I kept at it. I remember trying to pull family and friends along to spread the wealth and risk, but more times than not, these efforts met with fruitless results. I didn't let this stop me, though; don't let this stop you from moving ahead either. It is your actions—not the actions of others—that will make sure you get there. Let me be clear. This book is truly about many things, mainly:

- *Life*
- *Mindset*
- *Journey*
- *Planning*
- *Empowerment*
- *Change*
- *Wealth*
- *Goals*

This book is about all of these things, but even more so, it is about empowerment and you making a difference in your life, in the lives of others, and in the world by getting engaged and owning your future.

CONTENTS

PREFACE

This book is for you. Get these concepts down and do what you can to act on the information and to correct your course for you, your family, the people around you, and those who will come after you. This book is about financially getting there and actively pursuing things that will help you on your journey to individual economic empowerment. This book should be a quick read and could be read in a day or two. It's designed to be read through and then reread again and again until you get it. Yes, it has some math and formulas and worksheets too. However, it is a book for you to enjoy, and hopefully you will come back to reread and engage the Do's.

I lost a lot of time while finishing this book. I started writing this book some time ago and intended to publish it many years ago. During this time, I had lost contact with the manuscript; it was stolen, a hard copy was misplaced, and the USB that a copy was on was also lost. But for some reason, during the many tribulations of this book's journey, it has found its way back to me. I took this as a sign that I needed to complete it and get it out into the readership environment. So here we are many years later.

Getting There is a book in which I have laid out for you a short, readable story. It is written to give you an understanding of where I am coming from. It is intended to set the stage for you, and hopefully conveys to you that if I can accomplish what I have written in this book, it can be done, and you can do it too. This book should give you an understanding that the choices we make while growing up and in our adult lives are the pushes and pulls that determine the progress of our journey to getting there. These pushes and pulls, right or wrong, are the direction you are moving in. If they are wrong and not corrected, they may hinder your trajectory to getting there. So read, adjust, and stay steady, and you will get there.

ACKNOWLEDGMENTS

This book is dedicated to those who went before me and those I had the pleasure of meeting along the way. To those who have advised and guided me right. To my dear friends and extended family. To my wonderful grandparents, Mom, Dad, and whole wide family, sisters, brother, uncles, aunts, cousins, nieces, and nephews—all deeply loved. To my beautiful "Darlingface" wife LaQuita, who has been a positive force in my life and has stuck by me all these many wonderful years of our marriage. To my in-laws mother Patricia and late father James, for having her and being a positive force for good. To my in-laws, brothers and sisters, aunts, uncles, and their families, for whom I wish the best life has to offer them. To my three wonderful kids who were the cutest, sweetest little babies I have ever seen. Well, that was then. They are all grown up now, and I can say they are wonderful, responsible adults. In fact, they are beautiful adults exploring and pursuing professional endeavors in their own way, trying to tap into the secrets of getting there too.

I would be remiss if I didn't say I love you all very much and hope where I was absent and where memories are faded that you know that you all are still cherished and greatly loved.

CHAPTER 1:
Introduction

First let me tell you that the main emphasis of this book is not about how many pages I can write, or how I can tell you a story or two about my life, or how I am trying to make it fighting against all kinds of odds. No, it's not. In fact, I want to make this book as simple and short as possible so that I get to the essence of what you need to know about the secrets of getting there—i.e., investing and creating your own "real" wealth. It is about respect, self-respect, self-reliance, hard work, and changing the old way of thinking about wealth. This old way of thinking about riches is based on debt, the things you have because of credit cards or loans. Thinking you have something, when in reality you may truly only have debt and misery, living paycheck to paycheck, and worrying about paying or getting out of the mess you're in is not the way to getting there. Looking the part doesn't cut it here.

This book is about getting there and following a plan to get you there. The goal of getting there is to arrive at a place where you can afford the cost of living and you have the ability to own what you want. It is financial security for life by getting in the game to secure, grow, and enjoy your wealth. This book is written by someone with no financial certification background, someone who is not licensed in the financial field or versed in financial law.

I do not claim to know the ins or outs or depth of what the financial professionals know. I'm just an ordinary person like most of you—a person who started saving and investing early on in my teens, a person who tried starting many small businesses like social clubs, music bands, a small investment group, and an international import business. I'm someone who has tried, failed, and tried again, someone still on a journey through life on a road that others have traveled well before me. I am an everyday person, married with adult children. My wife is a loving and caring woman who has been there for me, and I owe her and my children all my love.

I'm an ordinary person like you, fortunate enough to participate in life's journey, which has included being raised in a single-family home by my mother who also raised my seven siblings while working full-time. My father owned his own business, and unfortunately, through bad choices, he gave up ownership to others. He was away, married to someone else, so I saw him only occasionally. He was not that much a part of my daily life; however, he worked hard at his business and provided for his loving wife and my half-brother and sisters. On occasions when he would visit or when I would have the rare opportunity to visit with him, those times were rewarding and I will always cherish them. I could see my dad's work ethic, and I understood that he was a hard worker who was doing the best he could with what he had. He helped and provided somewhat for us, and, as far as I know, he financially contributed to our well-being.

My mother was the strength of the family. Although my mom worked full-time as an early childcare program owner, our family income wasn't that much. She provided for and took care of all her kids and ensured that we had food on the table and a clean home. She believed in hard work too, and we could see it each and every day. She got up early each morning and prepared us for our day. She was there to make sure we were ready for the day and there to ensure we went to bed at a decent time at night and that we were safe. She would cook, clean, stitch up clothing, and make sure we had the things that she could provide for us. She was there to teach us and nurture us through life as we grew up.

She kept us straight and honest and taught us right from wrong, and if she wasn't there, my brother or one of my six sisters would be there to ensure we were okay and we did the right thing. I was fortunate that I grew up with the values and morals transferred to me from my mother, father, my brother and sisters, and my family—i.e., my grandparents, aunts, uncles, cousins, etc. I am thankful for this foundation because it was the stepping stone that helped me graduate from high school, join the U.S. Air Force, complete college, and travel the world.

I must say that this for me was no small feat, because where I come from, growing up in the inner city of Philadelphia, there were many perils, temptations, and life-threatening challenges directly outside the door. I experienced many terrifying moments when my best friends or cousins or I, individually or together, had to choose between right and wrong, fight or flight during our daily life. However unreal, troublesome, and tough growing up was, my family's nurturing environment made me value hard work and to respect others, and it inspired me to be responsible, helpful, and a good person. If mom wasn't there, my loving sisters were. They collectively and singly steered me right, helped with growing up issues, and saved our lives during some scary, life-threatening events in our childhood.

I must say that although I have journeyed through many stages in my life, traveled the world, achieved degrees in communication, sociology/criminal justice and advanced degrees in business and management information systems, own multiple residential and commercial properties, and have multiple investments in stocks, bonds, and owner-operated businesses,

I am most thankful for my mother's sacrifice, my siblings, my whole family, and others who had a hand in helping me along the way. I honor and respect them dearly.

My wish is that you in your life's journey can be a force for good and that you can strengthen a good, nurturing environment for yourself, those you answer to, and those you are in charge of, among your family and friends, at work or at play. Be the source and force for good change.

Depending on where you are in your journey, you may have already accomplished far beyond what I've done, or you may just be getting started. I pause to say thanks, and I'm very lucky to have accomplished what I have. But my true purpose for stating this is only to convey to you, the reader, that (if you have not already) you too can and will achieve many accomplishments throughout your life's journey.

The secret is to get started and keep at it until forever. We all have adversity in our lives; yes, it will involve working hard and paying (more often than not) your own way. This is a creed you should hold dear because it will make getting there more true and rewarding to you. I tell you this because if I can do it, I know you can too. It does not matter where you are on your life's journey, this book is for you and for someone you know.

CHAPTER 2:

Mindset

When I talk about individual economic empowerment to effect lasting social change, I want you to tag on to this, a mindset of direct financial engagement and accomplishments. In other words, it is now and forever and has always been a person's mindset and how he or she sees through the noise that's designed to keep you struggling. Your mindset and your attitude are where it all starts, and making corrections in your attitude about getting there will set you on a course to truly make it. Your mindset and attitude are key. Why? Because the "I am going to be rich" mindset and the "I am going to make it" attitude strive to pay less and get a better return or value out of life and the things they purchase. The "I got to have it now" mindset and the "look at me" attitude tend to pay (in most cases) more. The "look at me, I've got to have it now" mindset tends to jump in regardless of cost, return, or value. Although individuals with this mindset can't afford a purchase or the negative life value attached to it, they still want it. Regardless of the loss to them, no obstacles will stop them from getting it. Hence, they end up making bad choices and in debt up to their eyeballs.

In other words, as I see it, the truly rich person's mindset pays far less money for the things they acquire (which is smart), while those with the "look at me, wanna-be" mindset will most likely pay much more money for the things they acquire (which is not smart), and therefore they will suffer and struggle more to get the things they want. They are more about showing off material possessions to those they think are watching them; all the while they are swimming in misery, their life and relationships are actually in shambles, and they are in heavy debt. They may enjoy looking like a big shot with a lot of material things for a few years or so. If they are enjoying evil-gotten gains or have gone on a credit spending binge, the fall is devastating—i.e., bankruptcy, jail, lost relationships, high levels of stress, and sickness trying to keep up with the Joneses, etc. They may even think someone is out to get them, so they try to run from place to place, but they sure can't hide. The long arm of karma or justice will catch up with them. Surely this is not a place or situation you want to be in or visit. If this is you, reading this book is a start, if you will, to getting you out of this misery trap and it may be the spark that helps you find a better way of truly becoming financially successful—i.e., "getting there."

One thing I can tell you that my mother and father told me time and time again is to save your money. Don't spend your money; save it and grow it for your future well-being. Consequently, I have tried to relate to my children again and again, when they were younger and now that they are young adults, to do the right thing, pay their taxes and stop spending and wanting this or that. I tell them to start saving more and growing their money so they can have and afford the things they need or want in the future. I continue to hope they listen and I hope that you too truly grasp and hold on to all of the concepts and lessons in this book. Don't get me wrong—we can spend and have the things we want too. However, we must understand that there is a method to acquiring the things we need first, then the things we want next. This book is setting up a path for you to come up with a plan and follow it for your future financial betterment.

As you go through this book, don't get bogged down with the math formulas I have included. Those math formulas are there for you to use as examples, not for you to stop and figure out on the spot what to do. In fact, depending on where you are on your life's journey, some of the information may not apply to you right now. It may in the future, however, so use and address what you can on those worksheets. Just correct them where you need to, so as to represent items in your life at the time you're completing your real entries. Remember you can always come back and get a better understanding of the ins and outs formulas or net worth charts. Just keep reading. The idea behind this book is to get you to save and invest. Read this book. Don't stop, keep reading, and act on the Do's as soon as possible. With this book, I'm trying to reach you or someone you know who can use this book, enjoy it, and hopefully put their future self and family in a better financial place because of it.

If I could tell my younger self something, I would say to stop spending and save, save, save, invest, invest, invest, open a small business, and grow my wealth. You have this opportunity now to tell your future self what to do and how to be prepared financially for your journey ahead. I suggest that you tell yourself now to stop spending and to save, invest, and plan. Reading this book is a start to developing that plan and may ensure that you are on the road to getting there.

The getting there concept is about your financial security and economic empowerment and about how you can truly effect positive societal change. Having the correct mindset about acquiring assets and money is where you need to be. Yes, assets and money—this is what this world and, by some small measure, this book is all about. It needs your enlistment and all positive efforts to increase your individual economic empowerment and to affect lasting social change.

What does this mean? Wake up and become a part of the solution now, not the problem. Stay in school, get better and more highly educated, skilled, talented and, ideally, become more successful in your life and show others the way to change our environment and conditions in life positively and forever.

CHAPTER 3:

Money, Money, Money

Have you ever heard the sayings "Money is the root of all evil," "Money can't buy you happiness," or "Money can't buy you love"? Or some other version of these? The bottom line seems to be that money is bad or evil and that you shouldn't have it.

How about the opposite viewpoint that money is good, in that if you have lots of it, you would buy a big fancy car and travel around the world? You would save the world, you would be set for life, or you would take care of your loved ones, and so on. I especially love that I would save the world. Wouldn't you if you could?

Well yes, money is all those things that are good for you, and it can enhance your life. It can also be bad and cause you to destroy your life and the lives connected to you. If money is not obtained, used, controlled, and managed correctly in a way that is ethical, great fear or harm could beset you. You may worry and be concerned that someone is coming to get you such as the authorities, your associates, the boogie man, or the tax man—i.e., the IRS. In fear over money is no way to live.

You must work hard for what you want out of life. Pay your way, and don't take from others that which is not yours. I say this because some bad actors out there think your hard-earned rewards are theirs to enjoy. Don't be one of them. Work honestly for your status, position, and financial success during your lifetime. In so doing, you are helping the overall efforts of economic empowerment, starting with yourself.

It is very wrong for someone to take what you have earned. In fact, when I was a kid, my sisters and I experienced this taking what's not yours in a frightening and unforgettable life-and-death event. You see, when someone takes what is not theirs, it hurts the owners and others connected to them in so many ways—e.g., their life savings, the funds needed for their health care or to help a loved one. As I stated, my sisters and I witnessed a direct, in-your-face attempt to do just that.

We were young kids growing up in North Philadelphia, Pennsylvania, in an upstairs, three-bedroom rental on a street lined with owner-operated businesses. As my mom has confirmed, one of those owner-operated businesses was on the floor below us—i.e., the bottom floor—and this store sold mainly television sets. Many different shops were located on our street selling candy, ice cream, groceries, and electronics. One store with a pinball machine was one of my favorite neighborhood stores, and it was a peanut store, where the owner roasted fresh peanuts every day. I enjoyed this store because of the pinball machine, but the store offered peanuts and other things too. And lucky for me, it was just a door or two away down the street from our apartment.

Our place was located on Germantown Avenue, with brick-lined streets, and where the trolley cars would run like clockwork each and every day. Reminiscing, the smell and taste of those peanuts were a very pleasant treat on most days.

During this time of my childhood, my family and I were just enjoying life and the things we had. One nice and beautiful day, my sisters and I decided to go down the street to another neighborhood store. When we got to the store, like kids, we dispersed immediately and went to our favorite areas of the store. I can remember smiling and thinking about the goodies I could buy with the money I had saved. Noise, music, talk, laughter, and a good hum were present in the air that day in that store.

All of a sudden, silence swept over the whole store. It felt like a gust of cold wind had shot through the store aisles, like a fast-moving train and the rush of air you feel in its wake. Then came the thunderous, crashing sound of something hitting a solid wall and out came a loud, strong, scary voice saying, "Give me the money." Mind you, while experiencing this in the moment, I realized that my older sister had already understood what was happening and she had gathered my other sister and me behind her. She was so fast her movements were completely unnoticed by me. I didn't know what had happened or how I came to be viewing this very frightening event taking place all while being fully shielded and protected by my older sister. My sister effortlessly moved across the aisles, gathered up her baby sister and brother, wrapped us up with her energy, stared the overbearing, angry man in the eyes, and said, "Mister, please don't. Leave us alone."

What happened next was so shocking we were not prepared for it. Now when thinking back on this event, I realize the store owner wasn't prepared either. This mean, angry person who took all the happiness and joy out of the day and could have taken it out for life. He turned his attention to us, and his red eyes, the steam of anger coming off of him, and his forward motion that seemed to be moving in our direction were all terrifying, but my sister stood firm. I witnessed this bad man's forward movement as he at the same time spoke directly to us, said "Sorry," and turned and took off out the door.

I'm telling you this because here was someone who was going to take something that was not his, and to this day I really don't know if he did, or if at that moment, he stopped and changed his course for the better and corrected the rest of his life. He could have affected the lives of all of us in that store in a very bad way, but he ultimately chose not to, for which I am very thankful.

He was making many decisions during this event. One of them was a financial decision—an attempted transaction that involved not earning but attempting to take someone else's hard-earned money. I don't know what he needed the money for: drugs, food for a family needing to eat, bills to pay, or just as a way to get rich quick. All of these are bad reasons to take what's not yours. Now, of course, you know that this is not the only way someone is trying to take what is not theirs; look out for bad money managers, money sharks, bad loans, shady investments, and so on. The takeaway is that loud angry voice ("Give me your money") in one's face isn't necessarily the only way people steal.

Bad actors try to take your hard-earned money in all kinds of ways. Do your research. Catch an episode of *American Greed*. Look up the Bernie Madoff (should be "Made Off" with other people's money) story and many others. Review and research the many examples out there and watch out and guard against being taken!

You have a choice—perhaps not as graphic as the choice the robber in the store had to make, but a choice nonetheless—this very moment to stop and change course and leave very bad financial decisions behind. As you are getting there, pay your taxes and stay on the ethical (good) path when earning, investing, using, controlling, and managing your money—that is, managing your finances as you accumulate your wealth. Yes, I said to pay your taxes and always do the right thing as you embark on your journey of getting there. Being ethical and doing the right thing will always reward you with peace of mind and a great feeling of accomplishment. That peace of mind will allow you to sleep at night and enjoy what you have accomplished. Wake up and always be respectful to others and yourself. Being respectful leads to more positive outcomes on your life's journey.

The phrase "money is the root of all evil" has been passed down through the ages. The statement is not taken lightly and has stymied many in their daily pursuit of financial independence. In turn, this negative position on money has restricted many from helping in the good fight of getting out of poverty, getting better educated, and getting better jobs. It has been used to stop individual economic empowerment so we can't effect positive lasting social change. "Money is the root of all evil" was delivered to me in a religious context claiming that money, if you have it, will lead you to become evil. Therefore, my psychological takeaway was: Don't seek money out—don't get it or accumulate it.

Stay with me here and understand the secret "do" concept. I know a lot of people are saying, "Now wait a minute" (when I say "religious believing" people, I mean those for whom going to church and praying are a big part of their daily lives). Why "religious believing?" I purposely use the word "religious" in this context because I believe all religions are grounded in faith, traditions, and prayer. People are taught to use prayer with the belief that by doing so their life will become better and that the things (health, riches, etc.) they pray for will become theirs only if they pray hard (harder) and believe (harder). God will bestow it upon them. Believers will be rewarded at some point here or in the next life.

Well, I'm here to tell you to believe in whatever you want to believe in and pray as hard as you want to pray. The answer to your prayer may get bestowed unto you. But you must act on what you are praying or thinking about. It is imperative that you understand this now—actions are required for you to succeed in your life's journey. Hence the word "do." It is an actionable word, and it should empower you to do something physically with material or any other desires or to overcome a challenge presented to you throughout your life's journey. Don't get me wrong. Love God and pray hard; however, God would want you to act.

Doing should not be settling, meaning, I got a job, I made one sale, I got one client, or two. Settling for I make x dollars an hour, a salary of x, or for I made $10,000 or $30,000 so now I can quit trying is something you should never do. Why? Because settling for where you are at with that job, pay, sales, clients, or a few thousand dollars will only serve to delay you. Be bold and brave, and go do more to increase your status, education, job position, pay, sales, clients, and dollars.

This is not about gambling or negotiating for a dollar or two. This is about you getting there. It's about you not settling for a few crumbs. Whether the goal is twenty-five sales in a day, four new clients in a month, or $1,000 more in savings and investments, strive to do better because you know it will put you in a much better place for you to be more and do more the next day and the next and the next and so on.

Know this now and keep this with you forever. "Getting there" is not a get-rich-quick event that will happen to you only if you can do this or that or if you pray. It is a work in progress, and it requires hard work, due diligence, perseverance, dedication, responsibility, and a long-term commitment on a personal journey to empowerment and to you getting there. I must tell you this other secret now because I can't hold it in any longer. It is something that can greatly improve your life and that is the ownership of being responsible.

You must understand that it is you who must have a sense of responsibility that incorporates consideration and fairness on your road to getting there. These attributes are the hallmarks of enjoying your life's journey that bring a true sense of fulfillment and success. You see, when you are responsible and when you are considerate and fair to others as you engage in your daily life, it is reciprocated throughout your lifetime without you even being aware of it. It can be the source of your big break. If nothing else, you are doing your part to make the world a better place.

What is this responsibility thing? How? Why? Remember that old saying: "The early bird gets the worm." Get up and get things done. Help out. Get to work on time, know your job, be kind and respectful to others, and contribute to your family's (team's) progress in as many ways as you can. Moreover, don't be a barrier to progress because just maybe one day it will be all yours—i.e., you may become the parent, owner, manager, CEO. Be responsible! Contribute to the growth and the success of your family, your team, and yourself.

This book is my way of continuing my journey, and it is my effort to fulfill my responsibility to you. More so, it is an effort to help empower and positively affect economic societal change. It is designed to be an easy and short read, a sort of "how to" book with actionable (do) requirements to help you start your financial journey to getting there. So read it many, many times until you get it. Purchase additional copies of this book, pass them on to friends and family to help them, and enjoy getting there!

You! Please get up! Get out of your way and out of any mess you may be in so you can be or continue to be a part of the solution and not the problem.

CHAPTER 4:

Secrets You Should Know

The two secrets of get started and keep at it are two of the most important things you must understand now in order to get (or finish) wherever you are going with your life's journey. This book is a start and should help you in some small way with the wealth part of your journey. It is not a complete map, neither is it intended to be. It is simple, practical, and intended to be as short and to the point as possible. In other words, the shorter the better.

If I could just say the number one secret is to get started and the number two secret is to keep at it, and that is all I needed to say, this would be the end of my book. It should be. However, if you are anything like me, you will want just a little more practical information on how to move forward and perhaps just a little insight on when is a good time to invest. After all, this book is about investing in your future and a kick-start down that path to financial security.

As you journey down this financial road, you must begin to build your wealth fortress and strengthen it with the two most powerful pillars that will withstand anything trying to break them down as you become more engaged with the financial world. These two pillars are your net worth and your credit score. Simply stated: You should work to get these two pillars higher and higher, and keep them there. Please research these two pillars (net worth and credit score) and request your free credit reports to boot. Yes, at the time of this writing, credit reports are free—so look into getting your free credit reports and get and review them as soon as you can.

Net worth is all the money and other assets (house, investments) you have. Net worth consists of inflows (assets, money) minus outflows i.e. liabilities and other money that you owe. In other words, your net worth is your assets subtracted from your liabilities. Assets – Liabilities = Net Worth. The higher your net worth, the better. Being house rich and cash poor with a high salary may not be the best indication of high net worth. It is the totality of your assets and debts. I will touch on this lightly in a later chapter.

Earlier, I mentioned a creed that is no secret, but it is a secret to getting there. This creed is the creed of working hard and paying your own way. Working hard is easy, right? Yes! However you want to look at it—I mean analyze it—you must take this to heart and work hard for what you want. In this instance, it means go out and do your homework on investing and building wealth. Research and search the Internet and listen to financial channels, radio, and podcasts for more information as questions come to you and your curiosity piques. At this point don't buy into money programs or money managers; get your footing first, then when you are ready, engage this pay-for-financial advice strategy or not. As of this writing, I have not paid for financial advice, neither have I gotten caught up in some type of get-rich-quick scheme or advertised program or some special must-have offer for the well-to-do.

As I stated, this is a quick "how-to" guide meant to help you get there by methods like saving, making a high income, and investing in the market. It truly does not represent the breadth of information on building wealth available to you. This book is just a little spark to get you started or to keep you going.

Paying your own way is a double-sided sharp sword, in that it is coupled with the secret of using someone else's money until and before it becomes a penalty to yourself. More about that later. For now, paying your own way involves—

1. Paying with your time
2. Researching investments
3. Reading books
4. Listening to financial broadcasting information
5. Making decisions on where to invest your money

While doing this, you may be paying out funds to purchase materials to better your understanding, which leads to you building a go-to source available to you for immediate enlightenment or enrichment. This book is a start, and paying your own way truly helps others. In fact, it's helping me to get there too. Thank you.

Wherever you are in life, paying your own way will purify the journey in front of you, making getting there rewarding to you. So no matter how you came by this book or your knowledge of finances or your success, please share it with others. By purchasing and gifting it to others and paying your way, you can rejoice in the knowledge that you may have directly helped lift someone else up. In saying this, go further and consider passing down a better financial situation to your loved ones which don't have to be within the family. I will speak a little more on this in a later chapter. For now, just know that it is truly your willingness to share, is the core essence of the full intent of this book—to change the paradigm and truly impact individual economic empowerment to effect lasting social change.

CHAPTER 5:

Investment Strategies

W hen is a good time to invest? The saying is timing is everything. Funny thing, though, they also say don't try to time the markets on Wall Street. Markets refers to financial activity with securities such as bonds, stocks, commodities, and other instruments of trade that are present in licensed and regulated facilities throughout the world. What are securities? Securities are financial instruments—one is bonds, which are in the debt category, and two is stocks, which are in the equities category.

1.   Bonds (debt category): Simply put, if you purchase bonds, they entitle you to the full payment of your principal (amount used for the purchase) plus any interest per the terms of the bond due you. You are basically loaning a company or a government money, and you expect to receive a return per the face value of the bond plus interest. The bond issued is sort of a promise that the bond issuers will pay you back. It is a debt to them that is payable to you at some future point in time. Examples include US bonds and corporate bonds.

2. Preferred and common stocks (equities category): Simply put, if you purchase stocks, you basically are buying a percentage (share) of a company—yes, ownership—and in most cases, certain voting rights and privileges to participate in the company's future growth, decisions, and direction.

See U.S. Department of The Treasury: https://home.treasury.gov/services/ bonds-and-securities for more information on bonds and stocks.

Other types in this category are instruments such as commodities, cryptocurrencies, index funds, mutual funds, exchange traded funds (ETFs), and the like. They are listed here but are out of the scope of this book. Please do your due diligence and look them up for a better understanding of their use. This book does not go in depth in these areas but gives them only a cursory mention so as to spark your interest and familiarize you with terms and other areas for your research. Each one of these categories has some risk. It is important that you have an understanding of the basic positions on risk.

Let's talk about risk. An old adage holds that the higher the risk, the greater the return. Yes, this may be true, and it is super fantastic if you win—the big lights, the noise and horn blowing, the people giving high fives, the people wanting to be your friend, the congratulations.

However, if you lose, you can say that the higher the risk, the greater the pain—the sad faces, the no eye contact, people saying that it's okay, that you can try again (No! Don't!), people getting away from you, people telling you to stay away because you're bad luck! That loss truly hurts in more ways than you think. And when you lose it all, people talk about you and don't want to know or be around you anymore. Even your best friends or relatives may disown you. Ouch!

Risk is like a challenge that is calling you. Take, for instance, two people with $1,000 each. One goes to buy lottery tickets and one goes to make a deposit into a savings or money market account. You know how this is going to go, right? The one who gambled the money, playing games of chance, finally will lose all of it. The one who saved the money still has it and may have made a little bit more. Yes, a little bit more—you see, there's this little thing called interest, and it adds to your money. It truly pays to save your money. On the other hand, gambling truly does not pay. Why? Because the odds are not in your favor and the risk of losing is high. So gamble if you want; however, this is not advisable. One thing you can be sure of is that the house always wins!

In addition to gambling, high-risk get-rich-quick schemes are surely designed to slow or stop you on your journey to getting there. Saving and investing in instruments are less risky and may have a more positive direct impact on your journey. Saving your money in an institution like a bank is less risky and will keep you on track to getting there and make it more rewarding. Saving and investing correctly will keep the odds on your side to ensure you are growing financially and help make your individual social economic empowerment successful.

Anything you do carries inherent risk. Saving and investing have associated risk too. However, chasing get-rich-quick schemes or pursuing games of chance—i.e., betting, time-shares, and other highly speculative endeavors are sure ways to slow getting there, and they can lead to something more devastating as in losing it all.

One may want to have a little fun. However, don't mistake wild speculations or gambling for the vehicle on the avenue that will get you there. More times than not, they won't. If you are engaged in this, watch out and don't crash and burn. You may win some, but remember the house always wins!

When investing in the stock market, watch out for that flashy, new, want-to-play, got-to-have-stock-too attitude. Do your research and don't get caught up in the moment. A steady investment strategy is best, and staying away from highly speculative investments is wise. Look up tulip mania and the dot-com bubble as two examples of wild speculations. During these two events, when you get right down to it, a lot of people engaged in speculative gambling. Sure, it wasn't rolling the dice, spinning the wheel, or playing poker, blackjack, and such. Nonetheless, people were jumping in and betting on speculative companies' earnings. The results were devastating for many of them. Don't be in this group.

We had the 2008 economy crash, and now we have 2020 COVID-19 economy and the wild fluctuations of the financial markets. So, here are some of the levels of risk that come with the securities, bonds, and stocks I touched on earlier. Bonds have risk. Did you know there are such things as junk bonds and triple A—i.e., "AAA" bonds—and ones in between? So when I talk about risk, I bet you can guess which one is more risky: junk or AAA bonds. If you guessed junk means junk (therefore, more risky) and AAA means outstanding (therefore, less risky), you are right.

Stocks have risk too. Some companies listed on the stock exchange may have internal and/or external issues that make their stock very volatile. Therefore, their stock is more risky than a more stable company's stock. Internal fighting, financial issues, insider trading, growth, cash flow issues, and local, national, and world events are all par for the course when investing in the financial markets.

Risk and reward are par for the course when working on your journey to getting there. Risk is something that you will deal with and have to come to terms with in this financial environment. It is something you will have to set a yardstick to and measure for your level of tolerance.

However, be forewarned that too high of a risk (as previously mentioned) could be devastating to your efforts to get there. Remember that risk is necessary, but risk is not your friend. Rewards are received in the form of interest, dividends, high FICA scores, low interest borrowing rates, and increasing investment portfolio and net worth. I will address this in later chapters.

CHAPTER 6:

Quick How To's

Here is an assignment for you, some homework, if you will. Go get four coffee cans, shoeboxes, or any four clean containers. They can also be virtual. Now label them "Black," "Red," "Green," and "Blue." This is important to get a visual representation of your financial situation. The colors represent the following:

1. Black: The black container is very good and where you will place/ identify funds that are not to be touched under any circumstances. Black is the chosen color for this container because, in the financial world, the phrase "in the black" is an indication that you or your company is doing something financially right with company growth and profits as reflected in the financial books. This container is long-term and is to be considered your retirement fund, an account for that day in the future when you are retired. This can be five, ten, twenty, or thirty-plus years out depending on your age and where you are financially today. Yes, this is a long time, but you must get started and continue to invest in this box throughout your working years. It is not to be used until such time as the date of your retirement and beyond. This can be your company's retirement account,

401(k), Roth IRAs, or your own self-employment retirement account that you have set up.

2. Red: The red box is your bills box, and it should include all your financial outgoes for the day, week, month, and year. The color red is chosen for this container because in the financial world, the phrase "in the red" is a negative and indicates (when written in red) that the amount is a negative from the account/funds you are working with. This is your outgoes and could be very bad for you, meaning this could slow or stop your progress to getting there.

An understanding is needed here; it could mean the difference between struggling (having too much going out) and making it (where you have some funds to spare) more readily apparent to you. Flagging your outgoes helps you identify areas in which you can cut spending, which could greatly enhance your chances of getting there.

The other two boxes you can label any color you like. The colors I've chosen here are green and blue.

3. Green: Green is your investment go-to money and it is to be used to invest in the market. Yes, the stock market. I will talk more about this later in this book. These funds will be put to use in investments that are more risky than normal savings accounts. Whatever you do, don't keep your money under the mattress or buried somewhere where it's not growing in value for you. Money must be invested or placed in a savings account to grow.

4. Blue: The blue box is your trash money box, and it is to be used for those things and pleasures you may want to indulge in on occasion. Hopefully, at this point you are thinking, "Blue box! Trash money! Indulgences!" At this time you should be saying, "Yea, right!!! This

will be rare for me or at least until I reach a milestone goal. It will be limited in use and should be more targeted to getting out of debt."

Of course these boxes are all symbolic of institutional places and services such as bank savings, checking, and money market accounts or other instruments such as individual retirement accounts (IRAs), certificates of deposit (CDs), and US or corporate bonds. So feel free to set up and secure your boxes or designate your current financial accounts as you see fit or as I have listed.

CHAPTER 7:

Goals You Need To Set

What about goals? This is a good time to set some goals, more so because goals will give you a target to reach for and make getting there only steps away. Our goals should be realistic and obtainable. They should be small enough to ensure that we get there but large enough to help in our journey. Write down what you consider to be your financial goal for getting there. Write down $5,000, $25,000, $50,000, $100,000, $500,000, $1,000,000, or whatever your goal is.

My getting there goal is ...

This number is your getting there goal. This number is your financial life goal, and so it will need to be large enough to make and keep you set financially for life. It may be a million dollars or two, three, or more, an amount that you think will support your future spending and lifestyle. I know I said to be realistic. A million dollars or maybe even a billion seems unrealistic. But truly a billion is realistic and reachable in one's lifetime. How? You can invent something, create an app, build and sell a very successful business, etc. I'm not going to list them here, but numerous examples exist of successful stories in print or on social media of people becoming multimillionaires or billionaires by working and growing their businesses. You may even know some of the names of the businesses they started, products they sell, or services their companies provide. You may even know of an invention that they created that made them a billionaire.

Just in case you don't get it, this is not about getting there quickly. It is not a (as the saying goes) get-rich-quick scheme. We are talking about long-term efforts and goals here, something you will be working on for a very long time, for years. In some cases, these efforts may take twenty to fifty-plus years—i.e., forever. So feel bold enough to write a large number that you are pledging to work toward while on your life's journey. Don't put down a billion just to put down a billion. Put down an amount that you truly pledge and plan to work toward until you accomplish it. You can say something like, "My current goal is in millions. I will work hard, trying diligently to follow my plan of getting there." Remember that this is a long-term effort.

When planning, a visual goal or timing structure may be helpful. Here is an example of something that could work for you:

1. Long-term goal: aims for something five-plus years in the future.
2. Short-term goal: aims for something twelve-plus months in the future.
3. Monthly goal: aims for something thirty days in the future.
4. Weekly goal: aims for something seven days in the future.

Ensure you set these goals and start to follow them as you pledged to do.

A simple pledge to yourself could be something like this:

PLEDGE

My pledge: I *(state your name)* pledge to set my stated long-term financial goal, which is *(state your goal amount)*. I pledge to do the hard work necessary: to earn, reduce spending, invest, and save to ensure that I reach my stated goal. By making this pledge, I am committed to accomplishing it within the time period I have specified.

If you stay true to yourself, you will make getting there happen. I have created this pledge sheet above and added one in the attachment section of this book. You are more than welcome to fill in the blanks and acknowledge your getting there pledge. It is important to do this because by doing so, you will affirm your commitment to yourself and the universe. Most of the times, if we commit to something and state that we are going to do it, it is more than likely that we will try our best to keep our word. So state your goal out loud and stick to it. Promise.

Here is a secret. I found out that setting smaller weekly or monthly goals will help you reach longer yearly goals. Note that all figures and amount totals that follow are just for illustration only and don't represent actual funds or financial positions of any real person.

Say I set a goal to have investments of $110,000 in five years. I know that I have to save and/or grow my investments by at least $22,000 a year to get there. How does this break down?

So let's say first: GOAL = $110,000 IN 5 YRS TIME

1. $110,000 (divided by) / 5 years = $22,000 each year

Checking it—$22,000 × 5 years = $110,000 check

I can then break this $22,000 down to a monthly amount that I would have to save or grow my investments.

1. $22,000 / 12 months = $1,833.33

Checking it—$1,833.33 × 12 = $22,000 check

I will have to save or grow my investments by $1833.33 a month to reach my goal. I can then break this down for the daily amount too.

1. $1,833.33 / 30 days = $61.111

Checking it—$61.111 × 30 = $1,833.33 check

I will need to save or grow my investments by $61.111 per day to reach my goal. If you reach your goal early, you can just reset your goal to a new amount and keep accumulating until you are blissfully satisfied.

Your goal (target) may be higher or lower than the amount listed above—this is not a problem; you can just plug in your numbers (regardless if they are higher or lower) to see your personal results. One very big caveat to your goal setting is that it is bounded by the level of funds and investments that you are currently working with. In other words, I can't say that I will have $110,000 and not do anything to ensure that I get there—i.e., save and invest aggressively, work for a promotion at my job, build a business, or do the proper things to increase my income and savings. How you accomplish these things is up to you, and setting on a course of action that is designed to get you there is a surefire way of going about it. Increasing your inflows and reducing your outflows are quick ways to start. In fact, because you are reading this book you have already started.

Here's more on planning. Again, to calculate the yearly, monthly, and daily dollar amounts you must save and/or grow your investments in order to attain your pledged goals:

Yearly:

Goal (G): $_____ (divided by /) number of years (NoY): ___yrs. = yearly goal amount (YGA) $ = dollars_____

Or: G/NoY = YGA$

Monthly:

Yearly goal amount (YGA): $__ / number of months (NoM): ____months = monthly goal amount (MGA) $ = dollars____

Or: YGA/NoM = MGA$

Daily:

Monthly goal amount (MGA): $___/ number of days (NoD): ___days = daily goal amount (DGA) $ = dollars_____

Or: MGA/NoD = DGA$

You can play with these numbers all you want—this is your way of seeing results and setting goals. It will give you the information you need to succeed. Now let's discuss how to get there without too much more fuss.

CHAPTER 8:

Plan (How to Get There)

First you must have a source of income and grow that income. Graduate from high school, college, or a technical school. Study for and get certifications. In some cases, you can get a technical or other certification in just a few weeks. Certifications are a good way to get started on a career path. The study and completion times could be of benefit and value to you. Get a job, get a better-paying job, stay on a job and get promoted, start a business, or go work for the government (local, state, or federal jobs) or a branch of the military. In addition, if you can, take on a side hustle or a second job. In fact, a secret to know is to have multiple sources of income and invest those funds into your getting there plan.

Once an income source is secured, if you are working for a company, invest in your company's retirement plan or open one of your own: 401(k), IRA, TSP, stock plan, etc., especially if they have a matching contribution. As a minimum, invest enough funds here to get you the company's matching contribution. This is basic and should be the first move you make to getting there. This is the black box I talked about earlier in this book. Diversify your holdings not only with your company's plans but also outside of your company's plans. In other words, don't keep all your financial eggs in one basket. Be mindful of just investing in your company's retirement plans. Diversifying is the way to go, and as you move through this book, other options will be presented to you.

The following "Your to Do's" are suggestions, and they are your choices, not mine or anyone else's. Always act on any information and advice from your understanding and your decisions to do or not or to invest or not. You are the one who is fully responsible, not me or anyone else. After you have done your due diligence and decided to invest in your company's retirement plans, an IRA, the stock market, or a business, remember it is you who is fully responsible for making that choice to invest in any financial vehicle, business, or the stock market. It is not anyone else's decision to make—it's yours alone. With that said, I caution you that the stock market can be a wild ride with various twists, turns, ups and downs, and highs and lows, which could have long periods of swings to the detriment of your positions and your getting there goals.

Hence the stock market is not for the faint of heart and not for gambling; it's not for funds you will need in a short time. The stock market is a long-term investment piece of your getting there puzzle. It is a must, and it has tax implications and investment allocation concerns. However, it is a must do. More on this later.

Do: Call your human resources (HR) department or check out your company's employees' investment/retirement information in person or online. Find out what you need to get started to invest in your company's retirement plans. Most HR departments have a wealth of information for you to read and study up on before you make a decision. Most of these plans have target dates and/or risk levels that you can choose to invest in—i.e., high, moderate, and low-risk investment options.

Within these plans you should select the level of risk and/or target date you are most comfortable with. As you invest through the years, remember to adjust your levels of risk as you see fit.

Move or adjust your allocations to fit your risk tolerance level as you grow your wealth. Please consider and explore any available self-adjusting reallocation plans, called target date funds. These funds are tied to a date on which the allocation will shift to a less risky strategy.

In other words, target date funds are pre-allocated named funds with an arranged date, normally years out, preset to adjust your investment as designated by the prospectus. For example, fund 2050, allocation 60% bonds, 20% small cap, 20% large cap, means that in the year 2050, the final allocation will be 60% bonds, 20% small cap, 20% large cap.

Before 2050, the funds in the 2050 fund may be allocated in a riskier way—i.e., 20% bonds, 20% small cap, 60% large cap. However, each year up to 2050, the risk allocation is changed and adjusted as designated by the funds' prospectus. Of course the target date funds are named this way because they target a future date—e.g., 2030, 2035, 2050, and so on.

SMALL CAPS are small companies with a financial capitalization of up to $2 billion. LARGE CAPS are large companies with a financial capitalization of $10 billion or more.

PROSPECTUS: The prospectus is basically an informational booklet that tells you all about the funds, fees, investment options, and objectives. In addition, it may have company and fund manager information.

The Source Investopedia.

Do: Contact your HR department about retirement plans. If your company doesn't have an employees' retirement plan, move to the next section and seek out a plan of your own.

Do: Contact a financial institution of your choice and ask about IRAs. Don't pay for this service. Someone should be able to discuss this free of charge. If not, go to another advisor or research how to set up an IRA.

Do: Research the company's offered plans—get their prospectus and look at the growth of the plans. Look at where any dollar amount (usually $10,000) has grown over five or ten years or since the inception period. Look at the historical fund price chart, the rate of return, and fees you pay to own the fund. Always compare plans before investing.

Most plans will show you the growth chart of a certain amount of money (normally $10,000, but it can be more or less) during a number of years. This will give you a visual of where (if you had invested at year x) your funds have decreased or increased during that time as presented by the chart.

Based on the type of fund, you should be able to calculate the level of risk by reading the prospectus. Armed with that information:

Do: Select your level of risk. High-risk investments are most likely volatile, with up-and-down swings. The younger you are, the more time you have to recover losses. However, I would not rule this risk level out at any age. I would, though, be prudent with the amount (percentage) that I invest here at any age.

Moderate-risk investments are less volatile. This level is safer and does add some risk, but it can lead to a steady, medium level of return on your investment. This level may help your portfolio keep up with or surpass inflation. What is inflation? Inflation is something like the cost of goods you pay now versus what you will pay in the future. Let's say you can buy a cup of coffee today for $3.50 and a year from now that same cup of coffee costs $5.50. For a simple understanding here, let's use your investment (savings, money market, etc.) returns (interest, dividends—i.e., profits) to pay for that coffee now and in the future. Say your investments today returned $3.50 to you—i.e., interest or dividends paid to you from your investments. You can afford to buy that coffee today. Now in the future, let's say your investment (interest and dividends) returned $4.00 to you. You can't buy that coffee a year from now at $5.50—your investment returns (interest or dividends) did not keep up with inflation.

This is a prime example of why you must invest. You can't keep your money in your pocket or purse, hidden under the mattress, or buried because the face value will be the same as at the time you placed it in that hidden place. In fact, the worth may have diminished greatly, and the cost to buy present-day goods will just eat up what you have stored away.

I know this is a simple way to look at this. However, the takeaway is that coffee, as with other things we purchase, will most likely cost more out of pocket in future years. Therefore your money must grow at the same rate or preferably more, much higher than inflation so that you can afford the things you want to buy later on, down the road.

Low-risk investments are more stable than the others, with the lowest level of return to you. They are stable and should be the safest offerings your company or self-directed investment plan has available for you. You should invest some here—if not for a safe haven and diversification of your funds, for peace of mind. Do take to heart the inflation effect. Your money must grow by at least the rate of inflation to be on par with the cost of goods or cost of living down the road. Low risk is a safer investment category to be in, but it could have a very minimum return to you. It is your call, but a small amount (percentage) here with higher adjustments as you get older or as your concerns about riskier options grow is perhaps the way to go.

CHAPTER 9:

You Must Do the Do's

D o invest in the company or self-directed plan of your choice at your comfortable risk level. Put some funds in high-risk investments and some in moderate to low-risk investments; you choose the percentage. This is a must and I cannot stress this enough—if your company has a retirement plan match, more so if it will match and add a percentage of money to what you are investing, then invest in your company's retirement plan up to the match because it's like extra money to you. Or open and invest in a self-directed retirement plan, an IRA. After your research is completed and your comfort risk level is decided, select the plan and start contributing a percentage of your pay each payday to it. Secret, did you know that the funds you invest in a traditional IRA are not taxed when they are invested into your retirement account? That's right: the full amount is invested and is not taxed until you withdraw it many years later. However, read up on the time period and age of retirement before withdrawing funds because there is a penalty for early funds withdrawal. What? A penalty to use your money? Yes (normally before age fifty-nine and a half). Remember this investment is long-term and is in your black box. So don't be afraid of the age restriction penalty. You should invest funds in this box.

Say you invested $1,000 in your traditional IRA retirement fund. That full $1,000 will be deposited and will go to work for you immediately. On the other hand, if it was taxed before investing, say even by $10 (we know that the taxes would be much higher), then only $990 would go to work for you. This is a reduction in what you have working for you and will make a difference in what you could have earned throughout the years your funds were invested. However, with a traditional IRA (investing with before [pre] tax dollars), at the point of withdrawal, the amount you are withdrawing will be taxed at your current tax rate. When you withdraw funds from this account is when you are taxed on the amount you withdraw.

I don't know if you have heard of a method of investing that uses taxed (at your current tax rate) funds to invest so that when you are ready to take distribution (withdrawals) that money will not be taxed again. This is a clever way to not pay future taxes on money that you earned today. Since you already paid at your current tax rate, you can forgo paying any federal taxes on your future investment profits. Look into Roth IRAs. If you think your tax rate will be higher or that taxes will go up in the future, maybe this type of instrument is best for you. In any event, invest. More so, diversify your investments and enjoy watching the fruits of your labor add up as you move forward on your journey to getting there.

Roth IRA caveats include that you can make "anytime" withdrawals before age fifty-nine and a half (only up to the amount you invested) without paying taxes. However, you can't withdraw more funds than you invested without those extra funds being penalized or being penalized for early withdrawal of funds above your principal amount invested. There are some other caveats that you may need to know, so if you are interested in this type of investment, then please research Roth IRAs further.

Roth IRAs are after tax dollars and traditional IRAs are before tax dollars that will be used to invest. Depending on your future position, one may be better than the other. You can allot a little to both if you want. This way as you get more familiar with these investment vehicles and begin to better understand your plan, you then can make adjustments as you see fit. Your plan may consist of a company's baskets of funds or individual stock, mutual funds, or ETFs of your own choosing.

Do – Get a savings or money market account—this will be used later on and will be required for more direct stock market investing. You know that this too is one of the things you should have in your getting there chest. It is required that you have a savings or money market account from a bank or credit union that charges "no fees" for their services—especially withdrawals. Check out the differences of each, but basically look for the one that pays higher interest (a good thing) to you than the others.

However, compare them because one may have more limits and fees than the other. So be sure to shop and research each and pick the one that's best for you. Be sure to pick one that is insured (at no cost to you) by the Federal Deposit Insurance Corporation (FDIC). This is normally indicated by a statement such as "a member of FDIC"; this way you can rest assured that your funds in that institution account (up to a specified dollar amount) are safe and protected by the full faith of the US government.

This account should be separate from anything else you have and not a part of your regular savings or checking accounts. If you have an account already, designate it as your investment account or get another one at a different bank if you have to. This account is exclusively for market investing. It will be linked to your online brokerage account and should not be the account that you have all of your hard-earned money in or the account you have been doing business as usual with, at least not initially if at all.

My concern on this is some of you may be rightfully afraid of linking your hard-earned money account to a brokerage firm for investing in the stock market. Opening this separate account and designating it as your market investment account should give you more control and allay fears that your primary funds are not linked. It will in turn allow you to establish a link with most online brokerage firms for immediate investment of the funds you designate and transfer. In other words, it will allow you to move funds as needed to and from your accounts much more conveniently, timely, and safely, and at no cost to you.

Secret – You can transfer funds from your bank without a fee. Check with your bank and make sure you are using the process that doesn't cost you a penny to move funds from one account to another. Usually, wire transfers will cost you a fee and the funds will be in your account the same or no later than the next business day. However, the other, free transfer method will have your funds available within three business days. This works for me. Both will require basic information and the routing and account numbers to link the accounts.

Ensure the account you choose to use can be linked to your brokerage account. Some brokerages may allow you to link credit cards. I caution you here to be careful, and if you do link credit cards to your accounts, avoid getting caught up in purchasing and investing with funds you really don't have. It could lead to you owing more debt than is worth it. "Credit carding" your way is hazardous to your getting there. Until you are in full control of your funds and can pay off your credit card in full each and every month, don't do it. Use funds you have available to start and grow your investments. Only use targeted funds that are designated by you and that you are comfortable with investing. Keep away from margin, lent, borrowed, and payday loans—i.e., high-interest borrowing that you will have to pay back at the designated date (days, weeks, etc.) in the future.

CHAPTER 10:

Do Ins and Outs

D o: Write down your outflows. Here is an exercise you must do. Go to your computer, phone, or any device, or get a pen/pencil and piece of paper if you have to. Now let's do some hard work. Start writing down everything that you spend your money on—i.e., bills, rent/mortgage, utilities, gas for the car, eating out, partying, school, vacation, etc. I have listed below an example of items someone may have a responsibility for. These examples are for illustration purposes only and are not reflective of actual funds, accounts, or real account holders' expenses.

Example: Outflows (Debt/Expenses)

Mortgage Loan (MLND)	$125,000 (for net worth)
Mortgage Payment (MP)	$900 monthly
Car Loan (CLND)	$30,000 (for net worth)
Car Payment (CP)	$250 monthly
All Credit Cards Accounts (ACCND)	$20,000 (for net worth)
Credit Card Payment (CCP)	$300 monthly
Eating Out (Partying) (EO)	$300 weekly
Water Bill (WB)	$90 monthly
Cable TV (CTV)	$120 monthly

Gas (Vehicle) (GAS)	$120 weekly
Phone (PH)	$80 monthly
Internet Service Provider (ISP)	$55 monthly
Coffee (C)	$7 day × 20 days = $140
Lunch (L)	$9 day × 20 days = $180
Staples (Food) (S)	$300 biweekly × 2 = $600
Shopping for Clothing (SC)	$150 weekly × 4 = $600

Did you notice the "net worth" tags in these examples? I'm going to list those tagged net worth items as listed in the examples:

Tagged net worth items: Owed Asset Debt (D)

(D) Mortgage Loan MLND	$125,000
(D) Car Loan CLND	$30,000
(D) All Credit Cards Accounts ACCND	$20,000
Total Assets Debt	$175,000

Example: listed outflows items (expenses only—i.e., what you pay out [bills] each month)

(OUT) Mortgage Payment (MP)	$900 MP
(OUT) Phone (PH)	$80 PH
(OUT) Car Payment (CP)	$250 CP
(OUT) Internet Service Provider (ISP)	$55 ISP
(OUT) Credit Cards (CCP) Payment	$300 CCP
(OUT) Coffee (C)	$140 C
(OUT) Eating Out (Partying) (EO)	$1,200 EO
(OUT) Lunch (L)	$180 L
(OUT) Water Bill (WB)	$90 WB
(OUT) Staples (Food) (S)	$600 S
(OUT) Cable TV (CTV)	$120 CTV
(OUT) Shopping for Clothing (SC)	$600 SC

(OUT) Gas (Vehicle) (GAS)	$480 GAS
TOTAL: Outflows	$4,995

Outflows: The more detailed you are here, the more likely you will be able to spot areas of waste and abuse by you or perhaps others. Doing this exercise will arm you with a visual, in-your-face wealth of information that should compel you to make the necessary corrections that will have a positive impact on your journey to getting there. Trying to keep up with the Joneses, movies/music stars, or sports figures by dressing, looking like, or buying the things the Joneses or celebrities buy only serves to increase your outflows. Most of these celebrity figures are paid to sell clothes, makeup, shoes, etc. Don't get caught up in this look-at-me environment pushing you to financial ruin. Be as detailed as possible and don't worry; you can always come back and amend any area on this as you go. However, I must stress that the more you know about your outflows, the better armed you will be to make corrections.

Here's a secret—STOP IT!—outflows are a killer. They are very sneaky, they are everywhere, and no matter what you do, they will be there time and time again. They will sink your efforts to get there and will cause you to think that whatever you are spending your money on is the thing you need to be spending your money on. It is not! These are outflows that you need to get a handle on. Let me be clear: "outflows" are anything and everything that you are spending on, no matter what it is. That coffee, lunch, car, trip, that new shiny thing—whatever. STOP! Funnel those funds into getting there. Do you really need it, or do you just want it because you have the "look at me" syndrome?

Write down what you own and your inflows. Here is a secret. You should have multiple sources of income—not to use to buy what you want now but to invest and save for what you can have much later down the road. Implementing this one little secret will greatly increase your chances of getting there.

What are multiple sources of income? These can include taking side jobs, selling items on one of the social media stores, hosting a dinner or car wash party, doing hair or nails, creating an application (app), or do some coaching if you can. Do a legal side hustle that brings in more cash to you. As I mentioned earlier, I grew up in Philadelphia, and back then most young adults and some kids were out trying to make a dollar. Each and every day this was the thing to do. We valued hard work and working for the funds we needed to advance us through the financial challenges life throws at you. I remember when my mom up and moved the family to a new house on Somerset Street, my efforts included running errands for my elderly neighbors, and I even packed groceries at the supermarket for any tips customers would give to me. During the winter months, I would shovel snow; I would take care of my own sidewalk, then I would go down my block, seeing if a neighbor needed help. In some cases, they did, and when I was done, I was most of the time rewarded with a few bucks. My reply was always, "No, thank you. I just wanted to help." The response was mostly, "No, Son, you earned it, and thank you." I then would say, "Thank you, Sir" or "Thank you, Ma'am" and I would move on to help elsewhere. Because of my up-bringing, I was really trying to be helpful, so it truly didn't matter to me to receive a few bucks, but I knew too that it was useless for me to refuse. So I was respectful and helped where I could and earned a little extra money at the same time. The message here is instead of thinking about what you can get or take, think about what you can contribute to help out your family and others.

I was lucky enough to get a paper route, and I delivered papers early before school each and every day. As a young kid, I took a bad, unwanted, unprofitable route that had one or two customers. The district owner (who controlled all the routes in a certain area) took a chance on me, and I grew that paper route into one of the largest profitable routes under his control.

At the time, I was engaged in a startup business (a business hustle) and other money-making endeavors too.

My cousin and I came up with a plan to make lots of money. He and I were always discussing legitimate ways of how to make money and how to increase our cash flow. We would talk about our future status and the things we wanted to have. During one of our many strategy conversations, we decided to look for new moneymaking ventures. So we set out one day and discovered that businessmen entering and exiting buses, trolleys, and trains, going to work in one of the many financial, law, and large retail businesses downtown were ripe to offer a service to. We also discovered that people out shopping may want what we had to offer. So, when we could, together or alone, we set out and sold any leftover newspapers I had from my paper route. I also did this before I went to school in the morning when I could, and I normally sold out just before I had to leave my post to get to school on time. However, Saturdays and Sundays were our most lucrative days. Go figure.

One Saturday afternoon, my cousin and I were down in my basement playing around and talking about the day, this and that. We then started to discuss other ways to address incoming money flows. So we came up with a plan and designed on a piece of paper a box (I'll tell what that box is in a minute). We then figured out what materials we needed to build this box and looked around my basement and found all the items we needed. We started to work on this box immediately, and after an hour or so, we had two identical boxes that we knew would bring us in more money.

With this box made, we would mostly set out on Saturdays, Sundays, and holidays together with our boxes and rake in the money. We made more than the return we made with the newspaper venture. On many occasions, our pockets and boxes were so full of cash that we would have to hurry home before some bad actor(s) would try to trick and threaten us in order to steal our hard-earned funds. I can hear them now. "Hey! Come here! Give me the money! Let's get them!"

On many occasions, my cousin and I had to run, hide, and get to safety away from some of the bullies on the corner or from other bad actors down the street who saw us and knew we were loaded. I can hear them now saying, "Those young kids! They don't need that money! GET THEM!" We ran time and time again.

As kids, we made a lot of money with that box. So much so that I saved up money and purchased a brand spanking new box with hinges and an indented rest, with all the supplies you needed inside. Did I say it closed too? My cousin and I were thinking about upping our game, even back then. I know my cousin and I had discussions about new boxes; I just can't remember if I purchased two or if he purchased his own with his proceeds. We were business minded even then, and we built those boxes by hand. We later invested in our equipment to better serve our customers and increase our profits.

Admittedly, the bad actors and bullies started looking for us, and we looked out for them too. We had to change our setup location constantly. We had to adjust on the fly, in the moment, because we never knew what life challenges would come our way. Guess what? We had to run more often and faster because we made so much more money. We found ways to protect what we had earned, and getting to a safe place was one of our most valuable lessons learned early on.

That box consisted of eight pieces of wood total, cut proportionally, two for the sides, two for the front and back, two for the bottom, and one for the front top lip, extending from the front top lip to the back. That shoeshine box made us a lot of money. I was able to upgrade my supplies and equipment and to save money in a bank savings account. I even saved up and bought a stereo system as well as supplies for the pool table I had.

That was back then. Today you have so many opportunities to build whatever you like. More so, today's wealth-building tools and platforms are plentiful—the Worldwide Web, with social media, blogging, podcast, online sales, publishing, coaching, investing, and the like. Find something, create something, start something in an effort to help you get there. Go ahead and do it—do something, and don't be afraid to fail. I wasn't. In fact, I failed a lot, but I never stopped trying. Go it alone if you have to. Just step up. I can tell you that going it alone is not that bad. You have a wealth of information and guidance at your fingertips. Just click search! Google it. This is not an endorsement of any search services, neither do I benefit from or share any liabilities for your results. Please be sure to understand any disclosure or privacy statements on anything that you do. Just use the search engine you are most comfortable with and search on subjects that interest you. Doing some research will make you better informed and greatly help with tackling or venturing out on your own.

Sometimes going it alone is best because when you try to include others, it may slow you down and prevent you from moving forward. Please take note of this, and don't let complacency or the "I need someone to do this with me" fears stop you from starting and helping yourself to get there.

Time and time again, I have tried to bring together friends and family. With family, I saw an opportunity to purchase an estate on twenty-plus acres of land at a very modest price. It was fresh, up-to-date, and big with enough room for you, me, yours, and others. You get what I mean. The estate had multiple buildings—i.e., guest quarters. This estate was going for a few hundred thousand dollars. I reached out and tried to include family members in this endeavor with a lot of upsides. It didn't happen, and that land is worth multimillions today. The area it is in has multimillion-dollar homes. Instead, going it alone, I invested in a nearby condo.

With a few friends, I wanted to start an investment company. The plan was to bring together equal partners and discuss wealth-building and investment opportunities. We were to start to accumulate funds through dues, planned events, or other investments as we grew.

We met a number of times, elected officers, had formal meetings, and discussed business proposals like purchasing real estate, becoming a single-source international essential oils distributor, and other growth opportunities. Unfortunately, the members couldn't see the need to contribute, invest, or further research investment proposals in order to propel us to a successful investment business. I recognized that the commitment from the other members was not there and my trying to pull them along was fruitless and would damage our brotherhood of friendship. We stopped meeting, the members went their own ways, and the effort to build an investment company was dissolved. That investment endeavor would most likely have generated multimillion-dollar investments. Surely by now we would have had assets in the millions under management.

I started my own investment efforts and I'm still at it today. I can tell you, though, that all of us are okay and each one of us is a highly regarded professional in our respective careers. Sometimes others are not in that entrepreneurial mindset, not ready for the challenge, or don't have the funds or time to participate. They may not be in tune with your vision and that's okay. Let it go, press on, and make it happen on your own.

CHAPTER 11:

The Assets and the Inflows

You can start assessing your inflows by writing down the funds you have coming in and the assets you own from all sources. This includes any income, investments, or assets such as—

Assets (+A) Inflows (IN)

(IN) Paycheck (PCK)	$1,000 month (Take home)
(IN) Side Hustle Business (SHB)	$300 month
(IN) Part-Time Job (PTJ)	$500 month
(+A) Investments (INV) (net worth)	$100,000
(IN) Investments/Dividends paid out to you (IDP)	$100 month
(+A) House Market Value (HMVN) (net worth)	$200,000
(+A) Car Value (CV) (net worth)	$12,000
(+A) Retirement Accounts Value (RAV) (net worth)	$400,000

Now target and pull out the income (IN) items (see listed below) to see the income coming in.

(IN) Paycheck (PCK) (Take home)	$1,000 month
(IN) Side Hustle Business (SHB)	$300 month
(IN) Part-Time Job (PTJ)	$500 month
(IN) Investments/Dividends paid out to you (IDP)	$100 (month)
(IN) Total Income	$1,900

Items designated net worth as listed above are pulled out and listed below.

LISTED NET WORTH ASSETS (Listed as [+A])

(+A) Investments (INV) (net worth)	$100,000
(+A) House Market Value (HMVN) (net worth)	$200,000
(+A) Car Value (CV) (net worth)	$12,000
(+A) Retirement Accounts Value (RAV) (net worth)	$400,000
(+A) Total	$712,000

Cash Flow Exercise

Now let's try to figure out the cash flow in this example. For this cash flow exercise, exclude/separate where net worth dollars are referenced. Now add all of the inflows referenced above and add all of the outflows referenced in *Chapter 10*. These are listed below for your reference.

Example: Listed Outflows Items (expenses only—i.e., what you pay out [bills] each month)

(OUT) Mortgage Payment (MP)	$900 MP
(OUT) Phone (PH)	$80 PH
(OUT) Car Payment (CP)	$250 CP
(OUT) Internet Service Provider (ISP)	$55 ISP
(OUT) Credit Cards (CCP) Payment	$300 CCP
(OUT) Coffee (C)	$140 C
(OUT) Eating Out (Partying) (EO)	$1,200 EO
(OUT) Lunch (L)	$180 L
(OUT) Water Bill (WB)	$90 WB
(OUT) Staples (Food) (S)	$600 S
(OUT) Cable TV (CTV)	$120 CTV
(OUT) Shopping for Clothing (SC)	$600 SC
(OUT) Gas (Vehicle) (GAS)	$480 GAS
TOTAL: Outflows =	$4,995

In other words, total the (IN) items up and then total the (OUT) items up. Don't add any net worth items in these two totals.

Get weekly totals for each; convert these totals to monthly totals by taking the weekly dollar amount and multiplying it by four. For example, Gas (Vehicle): $120 weekly would equal $120 x 4 = $480 monthly. Do this for all weekly dollar amounts you have, and use that monthly dollar amount for your calculations.

Calculating the cash flow of the listed example:

To calculate the cash flow, subtract the monthly outflows from the monthly inflows calculated earlier.

Monthly Outflows (MOF) = $4,995

Monthly Inflows (MIF) = $1,900

MIF – MOF = –$3,095

Monthly Cash Flow Total (MCFT) = Negative ($3,095)

Net Worth

You may be asking yourself, what about those items with net worth attached to them? All of those items designated as net worth do have a purpose. So let's talk about this net worth a little more here and do a net worth exercise using the provided example.

For your net worth

Use this as a guide: add up all your debt to include your loans—i.e., mortgage, car loans, and any other debt. Be sure not to add your loan payments into this calculation. For example, add only the amount you currently owe on your mortgage and not the payment. So add $125,000 to this calculation. The same goes for the car loan and other loans. Add where net worth is stated only.

Tagged Net Worth Items: Asset Debt Owed (D)

(D) Mortgage Loan (MLND)	$125,000
(D) Car Loan (CLND)	$30,000
(D) All Credit Cards Accounts (ACCND)	$20,000
Total Assets Debt	$175,000

On the inflows and assets side of the equation, you will need to add up the value of what you own—i.e., house value today, car value, investment value, etc. The truer the value, the more exact your net worth will be.

LISTED NET WORTH ASSETS—Listed as (+A)

(+A) Investments (INV) (net worth)	$100,000
(+A) House Market Value (HMVN) (net worth)	$200,000

(+A) Car Value (CV) (net worth)	$12,000
(+A) Retirement Accounts Value (RAV) (net worth)	$400,000
(+A) Total Value of Assets Owned =	$712,000

Your net worth (NW$) is calculated by subtracting your debts (what you owe) (D$) from your assets (what you own) (A$). In other words, A$ − D$ = NW$.

Debt (D)	−$175,000
Assets (+A)	+$712,000

Net worth (NW) $ = A$ − D$ = NW$ = $712,000 − $175,000 = $537,000 (For illustration only, this net worth is $537,000, more than half a million dollars.)

This total is your net worth, and it represents where you are financially in your life. If your net worth is negative, then you have a lot of work to do. If it is positive, you are in better shape. However, you too may have work to do, especially if you have not met your goals for getting there.

In fact, you must be honest with yourself and ask: did you account for all your debt/outflows? This is important because you need the true number to know where you are today. Recheck and make corrections if needed.

For more help on net worth and debt, visit the internet and search for net worth calculators. Select one of the returned search results to get an understanding of what you need and a simple way of calculating the numbers for yourself.

What follows is a **"working exercise on cutting waste"**:

(OUT) Mortgage Payment (MP)	$900 MP
(OUT) Phone (PH)	$80 PH
(OUT) Car Payment (CP)	$250 CP

(OUT) Internet Service Provider (ISP)	$55 ISP
(OUT) Credit Cards (CCP) Payment	$300 CCP
(OUT) Coffee (C)	$140 C
(OUT) Eating Out (Partying) (EO)	$1,200 EO
(OUT) Lunch (L)	$180 L
(OUT) Water Bill (WB)	$90 WB
(OUT) Staples (Food) (S)	$600 S
(OUT) Cable TV (CTV)	$120 CTV
(OUT) Shopping for Clothing (SC)	$600 SC
(OUT) Gas (Vehicle) (GAS)	$480 GAS
TOTAL: Outflows =	$4,995

Now adjust the outflows of $4,995 down to an amount that is much lower than the inflows of $1,900 Do you see it? Can you cut the overspending, the waste? Yes. Now please do this for yourself as needed.

CHAPTER 12:

More Money

I mentioned a secret earlier about multiple sources of income. Someone told me once that in order to get there you must have multiple sources of income. They were right. Multiple sources of income will help you in a major way to get there sooner. These sources should come from other investments and jobs you take on.

For example,

- Get a part-time job and use the extra funds to pay down debt or to increase savings and investment accounts. Paying off your debt is like giving yourself a pay raise. Why? Think about it. You don't have that debt payment (outflow) anymore, so that money is no longer coming out of your inflows, and you are no longer paying interest on that debt, so those extra interest payments are no longer outflows and are now back to you too.

Say you have a CC debt of $1,000 at an interest annualized percentage rate of 17%. So, for a simple explanation, the extra amount you will pay for 17% could be calculated by multiplying $(0.17) \times (\$1,000) = \$170$. This $170 is the extra cost for you to have this debt. Now we know that the payment is monthly, so $170 divided by 12 or $(170/12) = \$14.16$ would be the initial monthly amount you will pay extra for this debt. In other words, to have the debt and carry it to term will cost you more than the original $1,000. Simply put, $1,000 + $170 = $1,170.

Now we know that there are all kinds of credit and loan terms and many gymnastic ways in which lenders calculate your payment and interest amounts. However, the deep dive on term and loan payment calculations are out of the scope of this book. I'm just trying to simply convey here that the credit or loan amount of $1,000 plus any interest amount, in this case $170 or $14.16, that's added to your original debt amount will stop coming out of your funds once you get it paid off. That $1,000 is stopped and that extra $14.16 is stopped too. Or think of it this way: if you don't have this debt, you are not paying out this extra penalty. Remember, try to address debt before it becomes a penalty (fees, interest) to you. Now if you took that $14.16 that you are no longer paying out and put it in a savings or investment vehicle, it would grow and help with getting there.

- Buy your first house and have roommates (it's an investment) and get the homestead and mortgage tax deductions if available. Never buy at market value; buy something you can afford, and as you build equity you are improving your net worth.

- Buy a second house and have roommates or rent it out. Get the mortgage and other available tax deductions and get rent payments that at least equal or exceed the mortgage payments to include insurance and taxes if they are not included in the mortgage payments. Make sure you check on the going rent in the area and don't undercharge even to family members. If you want to give them a little break, do so; however, make sure you are still getting rent payments that equal or exceed the mortgage rate. Remember you are trying to get there and you may try to help a little where you can, but don't let helping stop your success. Help and engage with family but be careful. I was lucky in that I was capable of helping others. Don't forget to put your own oxygen mask on first before you overextend yourself in helping others. Remember that business is business and family relationships are family relationships. Don't mix the two.

Oxygen: Here is a better way to understand helping others. On an airplane the safety instructions tell you to take care of yourself first—i.e., put on your oxygen mask first—and then worry about others such as your child. The reason this is stated is to do with ensuring that you don't become a victim presenting another potential distress factor hampering the survival goals of many others. You not becoming a victim will increase the number of people capable of helping themselves up and out of the predicament they find themselves in. In other words, take care of yourself first (financially), then look back to help others as you become more capable and not before. This way, you can be counted on to be a part of the solution and not the problem, which is directly in line with your individual economic empowerment that will effect lasting social change.

Friends, acquaintances, and even family members who want help (financially) with their car, house, vacation, or expenses for things they can't afford. Hello! They simply can't afford them. Statements such as when I get a raise, you owe me, you can afford it, when I win the lottery, are all well-rehearsed. Instead, they should think about downsizing and stop buying things they can't truly pay for. Maybe they should live below their means so that when true hard times hit, they and you are better prepared to survive them.

I'm not saying don't give at all but give only very selectively and in other ways than financially—i.e., give advice, volunteer, donate items you don't need anymore, etc. You know the old saying: Give a person a fish to eat and they will be back time and time again for more. Teach them to fish and they will feed themselves and contribute to society for the betterment of us all. I may have got that all misquoted but the meaning is to stop creating dependency and start creating independence—i.e., where we teach and coach each other in life lessons so we can provide for ourselves and fully be prepared for our life's journey of getting there.

- Start a business and work to make it grow. This is an easy one if you can do it. It is one of the major routes to getting there. If your business endeavors are small, think big—i.e., think like you are a big business and act like it too. Always be professional and treat customers/ clients with respect. As soon as you can hire other professionals, do hire them and put them in positions that increase your growth and company profile. If you think big and always be professional, one day (if you're not already) you will be a well-established business machine.
- Invest in stocks, money market, CDs, and bonds and security instruments that pay you interest or dividends, and let this work for you by employing the method known as compounding. Compounding is something you will need to get involved in as immediately as possible.

Compounding is when your money is making more money on its own for you. How? Banks, money funds, bonds, etc., pay interest or dividends on the money you have invested in a particular instrument. This interest or dividend could be paid to you daily, monthly, or whatever the terms of payout are. Just leaving your funds alone sitting in the bank, bond, other funds to collect the interest/dividends paid by the bank, fund, or bond should increase the total amount you have available.

In other words, your total invested money will grow and grow for you without any new funds invested by you. It works too, but I would continue to add funds to help it grow faster. Seek out the institutions or instruments with the highest return possible and at the risk level you are comfortable with.

Let's look at a simple savings account. This account is paying interest/dividends of an annual percent rate (APR) of 0.50%. Let's say you have $5,000 in the bank and plan no additional deposits. You will, but this is just for illustration and not about the time/future value of money or complicated math. I'm just going to use a set amount and basic math, this will break down something like this:

Savings Account: $5,000

APR 0.50% = 0.0050

We can calculate the amount the savings will grow in one year:

Multiply the APR of 0.0050 by the $5,000 savings = $25

To then get the monthly amount, divide this by twelve:

Monthly: $25 divided by 12 = $2.08 per month

Now if we want to get this down to the day, we need to divide daily: 365 days into $25 = 0.0684.

This in turn means your money is at a minimum growing by 0.0684 each and every day. That's like seven cents a day for doing nothing. Your money is working for you—i.e., money working for money. I know seven cents doesn't sound like much, but this can be $700, $7,000, or whatever, because it depends on many factors—i.e., your principal amount and the interest to get the dollar amount getting paid to you.

But it gets better. Now throw in this method called compounding and your money is working harder for you. The day one amount of 0.0684 is added to your money and the calculation is then applied to the new total

($5,000.0684) amount (not just the $5,000) and recalculated each and every day, adding funds to your account while you sleep. Have you heard the term "passive income" or "making money while you sleep"? Well, this is it—you are making money while you sleep; of course, the amount you can make is based on the funds you have invested and the rates of returns you are getting from the selected financial firms holding your accounts.

Consequently, those interest/dividend rates can and do go up and down, so your funds will grow faster or slower depending on the rates' movements. Remember that savings accounts are normally secure, insured, and have low risk. So the rate of return may not be that great. Interest and dividends are mainly paid to you based on the term of the account your funds are in. Payment of interest/dividends could be daily, weekly, monthly (semi-yearly, bi-yearly, quarterly, yearly, etc.). Check the terms and you should be set.

However, if you want a more stable rate of return, you can lock in the current going rates by investing in instruments such as bonds or certificates of deposit (CDs). These instruments tell you up front what interest rate you can expect and under what terms (number of months or years) you will receive that rate over the course of the investment.

The CD rates are normally a little higher than the savings rates. However, CDs or bonds are less liquid than a savings account, and CDs or bonds "lock" your funds up based on the terms of the instrument you purchased.

"Liquid" is a term used to describe assets that can be immediately converted into cash. If you decide to cash in your CDs or bonds before the lock-up period ends, you will most likely incur a penalty (a reduction to the amount you will receive) perhaps on both the sale side and the tax side for early cashing out. Make sure you check the terms and your commitment before tying up your funds.

Money market funds are a hybrid of a checking account and CDs; generally, they pay a little more than a checking account and just a little less than CDs. They can be secure and insured, and they do not tie your funds up for any length of time. They are liquid.

Remember that liquid assets can be immediately converted into cash. So if you are planning on using your funds on a frequent basis, this is a good choice for you rather than the CD route. I would, however, check the terms and ensure that the money market account you use is FDIC insured. There are many financial institutions to choose from. I use a few different financial institutions. So as not to make any endorsements, I won't name any here. Do your own research and select one wisely.

CHAPTER 13:

What Does It All Mean?

This was supposed to be a quick read, so let me get back to the basics of this book—getting there—more specifically, investing in the stock market. How are you going to do that with the little (let alone extra) funds you may have? The secret is to stop spending. How are you supposed to do that, especially with all the buy this, buy that forces all around you, wanting and encouraging you to spend, spend, spend or to use credit, credit, credit— forces like your kids (if you have any), girlfriends, boyfriends, spouse, friends, and family, and the continuous barrage of consumer flashy videos, commercials, and other marketing materials telling you that you got to have this or that?

Stop your own brainwashing and stop the spending. Truly, it is as simple as that. You are on your way with the financial leverage pushing you closer to getting there. The secret is to STOP (spending), SAVE (your money), and INVEST (in your future). Remember I told you what my mother and dad always said—save your money. Start here, change your mindset, and STOP spending and save more.

Easier said than done, right? So here are some immediate things you can do to reduce your spending. Why? Because reducing your spending frees up more funds for saving and investing and will help to ensure that you get there sooner rather than later. If you don't do this now, then you will never get there at all. Don't count on winning the lottery or lucking into wealth. You will be highly disappointed with your future self. I tell you this now so that you can make a change wherever you are on your journey. Young or old, you can make a change to effect a positive outcome to your efforts at getting there. If you are young, make a correction; if you are old, get in control. This means that when you're young, you may have the time to make corrections and get on the right track early. When you are older, you need to get in control before it's too late.

A major step was picking up and reading this book. In fact, since you are at this point in the book, you may have already done the hard work and followed my instructions on writing down your outflows. No worries, remember you can always go back and complete those worksheets. With that done, you will have a head start in identifying those areas of spending that you can cut without issues. Some cuts may be harder choices than others, but you can do it. You must do it because this is all in the effort to ensure that as you are on this journey of getting there, you are prepared to make these hard choices each and every day.

Remember what the outflows were in our example: (well, here they are)

Outflows (Expenses)

(OUT) Mortgage Payment (MP)	$900 MP
(OUT) Phone (PH)	$80 PH
(OUT) Car Payment (CP)	$250 CP
(OUT) Internet Service Provider (ISP)	$55 ISP

(OUT) Credit Cards (CCP) Payment	$300 CCP
(OUT) Coffee (C)	$140 C
(OUT) Eating Out (Partying) (EO)	$1,200 EO
(OUT) Lunch (L)	$180 L
(OUT) Water Bill (WB)	$90 WB
(OUT) Staples (Food) (S)	$600 S
(OUT) Cable TV (CTV)	$120 CTV
(OUT) Shopping for Clothing (SC)	$600 SC
(OUT) Gas (Vehicle) (GAS)	$480 GAS
TOTAL: Outflows =	$4,995

We can start to take a hard look at where our money is going and where we can cut spending. Let's look at the easy ones first, say cable and other services like it. If you have multiple such services, reduce them (if not altogether get rid of them) down to the bare minimum. Do you have a landline phone and a mobile with all the available options? Reduce the phone services and research other options for mobile or landline phones. Choose one that does not cost you a high monthly fee. Call companies that you are paying for services, utilities, phone, and credit cards and ask them for low-cost options to reduce your bills.

THE "DO I NEED IT?" TEST AND WORKFLOW CHART

Do I need it—yes or no? Is it food, water, or shelter—yes or no? If no, reduce it or get rid of it. If yes—food and groceries—use coupons, buy on sale, and reduce spending on the most expensive food items where you can. Reduce your outflows in restaurants. Reduce spending on water and utilities by turning off the water when not in use. Do not just let the water run—fix drips and leaks immediately. Do not wash the car every day or take very long, overly excessive showers. Reduce spending on beverages as well—if you are paying for the restaurant, tickets, and/or rounds at the bar, stop. Look to rent at a

73

cheaper rate. Look at moving or downsizing if buying a house is not an option. Look into reducing your mortgage interest rate—look at your mortgage and get the lender to explain each item that makes up your monthly payment. Get rid of the mortgage insurance fee that protects the bank if you don't pay. Don't buy a big house. The cost to maintain a big house may be much more than you think and will eat away at your ability to fund your efforts at getting there.

Reduce other fees where you can. How? Talk to your lenders and the companies providing you with services. Tell them that you are looking to reduce your bill(s) and would like to know what suggestions they have for you and what they can do to help. Check your paperwork and bill statements and attack the fees and charges you are paying. Work to eliminate or greatly reduce them to your benefit.

For those who are afraid or on government assistance or just young or who are much further down the road and are reading this book, you can get there. You need to get a grip on yourself and where you are financially. Ask questions of yourself or whoever you have doing your finances.

Ask hard and sometimes uncomfortable questions like—How much is coming in for me from all sources? Where is it going? What am I paying for? Now mind you, this is not to get into an adversarial relationship with your-self (depressing) or the person you are working with. It is just to get a clear handle on where you are financially. Are you financially secure? Can you sustain your lifestyle, or are you relying on others, debt, or the government to keep you in the situation you are in?

Secret: Did you know that if you did your homework and opened a brokerage account, you can ask for an assessment of your finances—i.e., a retirement assessment? Never mind the name "retirement"; just work to get that assessment. It will help you gather up your financial information and when done, this assessment will give you recommendations on your risk tolerance and asset allocations.

You will receive a report with current and future projections of where you are. There may be a sales pitch for you to invest in the results as returned in the report. That is totally up to you not anyone else. You can just use the return report as your projections and investment suggestions. Some broker-ages will allow you to do your own, or other sites could do this. However, be safe and beware of who you are releasing your information to.

Sometimes we find ourselves needing help and would like to reach out to professional organizations. I must share with you something I came across from the *Moneyist*. In an article called "The Ethics and Etiquette of Your Financial Affairs," Quentin Fottrell shared this when advising a concerned, financially strapped person.

This person was seventy-three years old and was seeking advice on how to ask others (her relatives) for financial assistance from someone else's inher-itance. "Ask yourself what decisions you made that led you to where you are today and, more importantly, figure out how you can plan for your remaining years. You can enroll in Medicare, if you have not done so already. The AARP can help seniors find state and federal financial assistance and can point you to other organizations that can help with your financial, physical, and social needs. The Area Agency on Aging can direct you to local support in your state, and The Administration on Aging can help with housing, long-term care, and legal and financial advice."

State and federal financial assistance links: *www.aarp.org/aarp-foundation/our-work/income/info-2012/public-benefits-guide-senior-assistance1.html*

The Area Agency on Aging: *www.n4a.org/*

Administration on Aging: *https://acl.gov/*

Do I need to save and invest? As in the example, you can see that if the person would have saved/invested and prepared for life, she may not have needed to ask others for their inheritance. Don't become this person. Now would be the time to correct your course to avoid this possible future situation. More directly, do so by planning and preparing for your future financial well-being now.

I can go on and on and on like this, but I think you know what you must do. Stop spending! Once you have made adjustments and gained the upper hand, any and all savings returned to you (inflows) should be targeted to reducing bad debt and increasing the funds you have available to invest.

CHAPTER 14:

The Good, the Bad, and the You

Yes, there is such a thing as bad debt. It's that debt (a loan or credit cards) that just eats away at your finances without a return to you in the form of tax breaks or increase in value or monetary return once you own or sell an item. It depreciates (the item you purchased) in value, and you lose money each and every day you own it.

Say, for instance, that you get a car loan and buy a car. Most likely you will pay interest on this loan and will not get a tax write-off for it. Also, most likely when you go to sell it, you will not get the money you paid for it. The interest you are paying is money to the lender for letting you borrow the funds. That cost and the depreciation of the car's value is a costly financial mistake and one to avoid if at all possible. I know we need our cars but buy used and only what you can afford. Car loans are very bad loans. Not only do cars depreciate the minute you sign your name and are handed the keys, you will also pay through your teeth on the interest.

If you say you got the loan with no payment or interest for a few months or even a year or so. Well, it may be tacked on to the end or incorporated in the purchase price, and thus you are paying the interest anyway. Loans like these (credit cards too) are bad for you and will make you pay more for items that you think you are getting a bargain or a price break on. Those zero or free month/year terms are traps to make you pay more. So be careful of these loan tactics; they are designed to add more interest or penalties in the end, especially if you miss a payment. If you must use credit, remember the secret; pay it off before it becomes a penalty to you—i.e., extra interest payments and/or other fees tacked on to your original amount. Pay bad debt off as soon as possible. Pay credit cards off or pay the full monthly payment due before paying any interest and fees for having used that credit.

Secret: If you must use a credit card, be sure to get one that pays back points or gives cash back for using it. However, again remember to pay it off before any extra charges are added to your bill—i.e., pay the full monthly balance each and every month. If you can't do this, then don't put the purchase on your credit card. The big picture here is that maybe you can't afford it and really don't need it anyway. Let it go.

Secret: Pay the full balance due each month, and it will save you on interest payments and fees. If there is a fee to use a credit card, pay with cash or check to avoid paying anything extra. Did you get the secret? Pay it off before it becomes a penalty to you.

Good debt is debt that helps you in the process of saving your money and will return to you greater monetary value than bad debt—a mortgage, for instance. A mortgage loan will usually give you the advantage of writing off the interest you paid, insurance, taxes, and other expenses paid during that current tax year, thereby reducing your taxable income and saving you on the taxes you pay. It may even help increase your tax refund.

As tax laws change and you may or may not qualify, please check with a tax attorney/advisor/preparer to better understand what is deductible for your situation. If you need to have debt, then saving money on debt instruments (i.e., fees, interest, and/or penalties) is the way to go.

Secret: Good debt like an affordable mortgage will benefit you the most and, more importantly, it is one of your most important investments. So if you are looking to buy that car, here is a better option. Look at leveraging the equity in your house and buy used and only what you can afford, and enjoy a greater financial benefit to your bottom line.

Leveraging equity is not free money; it is only used so that the advantage is to you (i.e., a tax write-off) and not just to the lenders. Do not bite off more than you need or put yourself in a situation that reduces your efforts to get there. Your decisions are all made to reduce your outflows, not increase them. So be sure to look at the things you are doing and do what will do the least financial harm. Always consult with a professional and weigh your options before moving forward. Remember you are looking for the advantage and not the other way around—i.e., losing the advantage and paying much more than you need to. Always weigh the total cost of financial moves and make the best decision for you.

CHAPTER 15:

Trade to Stock Up

R esearch online discount brokers. Here is where due diligence is a must. Go online and search for online brokerage services. Pick out the main players—i.e., the ones that are secure and have been around for some time. I use e-Trade for all my personal trading. I also have a seldom-used account with Robinhood.

This is not an endorsement, so do your due diligence and check out other brokers. Look around their sites and check out other trading platforms. Check out how much it will cost you to make a trade. Most of these brokers are now allowing free trades to be executed on their platforms. Some of these discount brokers have very easy and accessible mobile applications (apps) that make investing easier, less stressful, and even fun to do. Please review a number of these brokers before you make your choice. Open two or so if you like. For this exercise, only one is our focus. If you already have one, then great; however, it doesn't hurt to do a review of these brokers' platforms at this time. If you do not have a device with online access, remember your local library may have free online systems for your use. Check it out.

"Trade" is the term used to express what you are doing with the stock— either you are buying (owning it) or selling it. Brokerage services normally have a similar feel on the information side of the house. But some have aggressive, fast-moving trading platforms that are in your face and that may be too much of a distraction to new users, so choose wisely according to your style. However, don't let bells and whistles scare you away.

One good thing is that the price to trade on most of them is not that far apart and mostly these services are free to trade, buy/sell stocks, mutual funds, and ETFs. However, make sure that you look at their rates and fees. Most online brokerage accounts also have no minimum opening deposit requirement.

If there is a minimum deposit requirement, but you like what you see, then meet their requirements and open an account. There is no excuse for you to not open an account with one of the many brokerage firms out there, one that's safe and secure. You can't say you don't have the money. With many of them requiring no minimum opening deposit, surely you can find one that you like. Do open one of your choosing.

Once you get started, check out ETFs and mutual funds. These instruments hold a basket of stocks. They have different fees, and some are higher than others. Mutual funds and ETFs can be managed or unmanaged funds. Check them out.

CHAPTER 16:

Stocks and Let's Do It Again

D o: No matter what research you have done—some, a lot, or none at all—open an account with an online discount broker. If you have done just a little homework on a discount broker and made your choice, good for you. Now open the account and relax.

That one is done. I hope you picked a good one. I'm not going to waste any time on this one because you will just need to follow the online application and complete the process to ensure that your account is open and accessible to you. Use the account information of the savings or money market account that you opened earlier and designated as the direct market investing account to apply, open, and fund your brokerage account. Follow the account linking process and link your brokerage investment account to your market investing account. If you get confused, call the customer service number and ask how to link your accounts.

Do: Buy stocks as listed on the stock market exchange. The New York Stock Exchange (NYSE) and the Nasdaq are two names you may have heard of and are the most noticeable US exchanges. Remember that a lot of up-and-down swings happen with stocks and the larger markets. There are also different tax costs with purchasing and selling stock. The objective is to buy low and when you sell, to sell high or for higher than the price for which you bought the stock. Also, for tax purposes, short-term means selling a stock that you owned for less than twelve months. Long-term means owning a stock for a year or more. Which would you pay more taxes on? You guessed it, the short-term (less than twelve months) stock. You will pay a higher tax on your profit if you were to sell it within a year. Look further into this and don't start day trading and you should be okay. Day trading is buying and selling securities within the same day.

Start off with whatever (small amount) you are comfortable investing. Buy stocks that you are familiar with. Do your research on the company first to see if it has financial, legal, or other issues that will signal to you to stay away. Do a search on the company; it must be publicly traded to be listed on the many stock market exchanges. Do your research and if you read something like company x is filing for bankruptcy, you might want to stay away. If you see something like company x's top management is selling off their stocks—in other words, bailing out—you might want to stay away. You must do your research on the companies you are investing in to ensure that you are not just throwing your investing funds away.

Normally, well-established companies that have been around for years are safer to invest in. More so, they are likely to pay out a dividend.

Dividend. What is that? A dividend-paying company pays out cash in the form of a dividend to holders of their stock as of x date. The x date signifies the date the company designates as the date you must own its stock to get the dividend. In other words, if the company announces that on January 1 of year x they will pay a dividend to all holders of the company's stock as of November 25 of year x, and if you bought shares of their stock on November 26 of year x or after that November 25 cutoff date, you will not receive the January 1 of year x payout. However, if you hold the stock, you will be subject to any future payout (after January 1) announcement dates based on your purchase date of stock x.

Conversely, if you bought on or before November 25 of year x, you will be awarded your new funds or new stocks on the stated date. Note that you can have the dividends paid in cash to your account or reinvested in the stock that will add to your stock's x holding.

Secret: I like dividend-paying stock companies. This type of investment is very good for getting there. In fact, dividend-paying (stock) companies help you grow your investment. This can be done by directing your brokerage account to reinvest the dividends into that company's stock, thereby adding more stocks to your account's portfolio. This is nice because this is passive investing where extra money is turned into more stocks and you didn't do anything but invest. Or, if you so choose, you can direct the dividends to be paid out in cash to your account. You then can use the cash to purchase or increase your holdings in another investment. Either way you go, dividend reinvesting is a great choice in my opinion; more often than not, it is the better way to go that greatly helps most directly with getting there.

Do: Consider buying into mutual funds and ETFs. Mutual funds and ETFs can be a grouping of stocks, bonds, etc. put together (grouped, if you will) by financial firms with a single exchange symbol assigned to them. This way, investors are not trying to track multiple symbols—they are collectively called some catchy name that may incorporate the fund's holdings. A fund manager or team manages the percentage of or the weight of investing the available funds into securities as listed in the funds' prospectus/brochure. Investors have very little say in the investment choices (maybe during proxy voting); however, they mostly have no say on how the total funds will be invested.

Most mutual funds and ETFs have ongoing management and/or other fund-related fees that could cause you to lose or slow your growth to getting there more than you think. You must understand these costs and come to a conclusion as to whether investing in mutual funds or ETFs is right for you. I tend to like no-cost or low-cost (fees) mutual funds and ETFs and have a few in my portfolio too.

Secret: Look at load and no-load funds and be sure to understand the back-end, front-end, and other fees associated with mutual funds before you invest. I have both, and I much favor the no-load over the loaded funds any day. Always be mindful of management fees and compare fees with like funds to get an understanding of risk and future returns.

CHAPTER 17:

Just a note to self – Estate Plan: Wills & Trusts

O kay, now with all this planning and investing going on, we really need to get something straight which is if you have any money, a couple of dollars, (no matter where it is, i.e under a mattress or in a hole) or own anything then you have an estate. So once and for all let's dispel the notion that only the rich have an estate. Guess what? You do too. Because you have been working on, or, have completed the Do's in this book, you now know more about the size of your estate. That early planning you did has armed you with a wealth of information on the state of your affairs. You are now more ready to address and better strengthen your getting there efforts and secure the way forward for others. Think of it this way; since you can't take it with you, leaving a legacy behind to help support the family is a better way to go.

To do this, you must get at least a Will completed. More so, because you may want to consider passing down a better financial situation to your loved ones to help advance those you are leaving behind. Or, as a safeguard to financially insure someone can help you. Be mindful of who this person is. Entrust in someone that has shown respect to you. Is there for you, helped out, responsible to you, and is helping to advance the family/team goals. If this is not a family member, i.e. your children, or other family members, then look to others perhaps your grandchildren for this planning requirement.

Estate planning; Wills and Trusts, (which are out of the scope of this book) is worth looking into and will greatly help you in this area. It will give a better understanding on how to leave a legacy and to ensure your wishes are carried out. Get a Will completed. While living, ensure that you balance and control your estate the way you want it to be. Then ensure your Will reflects your desire. This will help in many ways with taxes, and reduce the confusion on what you intend to do with your estate.

I've heard a firsthand account of a family fighting over their inheritance interest. All to common statements such as; it's mine, it's in my name, it's intended for me, led to an all-out physical fight. Brothers, wives and other family members, were at each other's throat over what each was to receive upon the future death of their father. As this story was told in detail, I envisioned steam coming from each family member, eyes turning fire red, hate, pots, pans, broom sticks, knives, guns, hair pulling, screaming, all kinds of loud swear words and punches getting thrown about. As one of the participants was telling me of the very disturbing event he was involved in, I was truly amazed that the father was still alive and mentally and physically active. This family's hurtful and horrible event was all over a single family item that one brother wanted and the other thought would be his upon the future death of their father. Mind you this is happening while the father is present and still actively enjoying his life. Now imagine what could playout when he is no longer here.

Consequently, don't believe your situation (family) is different, and that this can't happen in your presence (while you are living) or when you are no longer here – it truly can. So, thinking someone will do the right thing, is not the way to leave your estate. Be aware of; misguided controlling manipulations of, it's mine, it was intended for me, situations in your estate affairs. You must spell out your wishes to your loved ones to avoid infighting, mistrust, or hate that will lead to the destruction of family relationships and your financial legacy.

Wills and trusts can be very complicated, so you should look further into this with a legal professional. Get advice to understand what you need to have or do to make sure your wishes get completed as you instructed. Seek out a free consultation with an estate planning attorney in your area to better understand the cost and your needs. As a minimum, work with them to get a Will completed and the power of attorneys for your medical and financial decisions in case you become incapacitated and can't make these decisions for yourself.

EPILOGUE:

Intent – Piecing It Together

Overall this book contains a wealth of information. Please read and reread it for the best ways forward to your journey to getting there. It is not all it can be, but it is a start for most of us who wonder how to make it in this world. I can tell you this: no matter what you have been told, any path you choose will require hard work, goal setting, sticking to it, and learning. Increasing your financial knowledge will always be a part of that journey to getting there. Understand that, no matter what, these elements in this book will always be a part of your journey.

I hope in some small way this reading has given you a spark to get started now. This book is not intended to tell you everything there is about this or that, what is meant here or there. It is intended to do one thing, and that is to get you moving toward getting there by doing. Get started now.

For legal and financial reasons, I am neither endorsing nor identifying many of the names of people, businesses, or products mentioned in this book. I am purposely leaving this up to you, the reader, to do your own due diligence and further research to better your understanding of investing before you invest your hard-earned money into more risky investments.

Consequently, you have not seen a lot of the names of stocks, bonds, mutual funds, brokers, banks, or other products in this book. If something has slipped through, it is un-intentional and has neither the ring of endorsement nor the intent to credit or discredit those so named. I am not receiving compensation from any names that may have slipped in this book.

This book is only a start, and it is not by any means complete on any financial subject. I hope as stated that this book is the spark that gets you going and helps you in some small way on your journey to getting there. If by chance it does help you, I encourage you to help someone else and purchase them a copy of this book. This book should be required reading for those who are looking to get there. I think that's all of us.

Remember that it is the choices you are making now that will get you the future you want tomorrow, so make wise and responsible choices starting today. Getting there is a part of the solution and will ensure that you are doing the right thing with helping the world correct the current economic societal disparities and stop them in the future. In other words, your individual economic empowerment will effect lasting social change. Coupled with your respect for others and your willingness to be a part of the solution to combat economic injustice, now and in the future, will ensure a more impactful, equitable, and positive societal change.

No matter the information in this book, I want you to start investing now! Get to it! Jump in now, start with $10 or $100—something small—and learn, build, and get better as you go. Don't hesitate. You don't have to know it all before you start. I would tell you to start investing now. Please do.

Thank you for reading this book, and good luck on your journey to getting there!

ATTACHMENT #1

My Pledge

I *(state your name)* pledge to set my stated long-term financial goal, which is *(state goal amount)*. I pledge to do the hard work and ongoing research necessary to help me employ the tools to help me on my journey of getting there. I pledge to earn as much as I can, I pledge to reduce my spending, invest, and save to ensure that I reach my stated goal. By making this pledge I am committing myself to accomplishing it. I pledge to stay true to myself to ensure I make getting there a fulfilling reality.

These words are my bond.

Signed: _____

REFERENCES

1. U.S. Department of The Treasury: https://home.treasury.gov/services/bonds-and-securities

2. Wikipedia page finance: https://en.wikipedia.org/wiki/Finance

3. Federal Deposit Insurance Corporation page on insurance: www.fdic.gov

4. *The Moneyist*. "My uncle left his kids $3 million and left me $15,000. I'm 73 and not in good health. Is it wrong to ask my cousin for another $5,000?" Published September 14, 2020 at 11:01 a.m. ET by Quentin Fottrell. Here: https://www.marketwatch.com/story/my-uncle-left-his-kids-3-million-and-left-me-15000-im-73-and-not-in-good-health-is-it-wrong-to-ask-my-cousin-for-another-5000-2020-09-09

5. Yahoo Business/Finance news and market activities: https://finance.yahoo.com/

6. Google Search

7. The Millionaire (Series) Mind by Tom Stanley (Reading suggestion)

8. The Richest man in Babylon by George S. Clason (Reading suggestion)

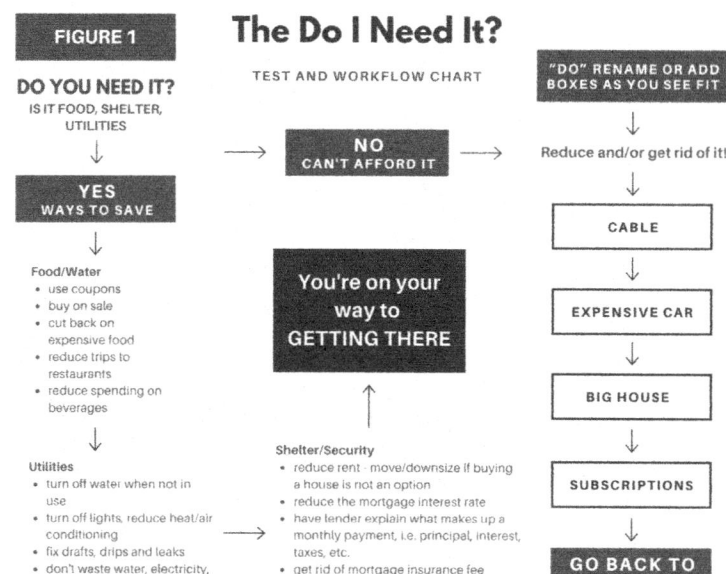

The Do I Need It?

FIGURE 1

TEST AND WORKFLOW CHART

DO YOU NEED IT?
IS IT FOOD, SHELTER, UTILITIES

↓

YES
WAYS TO SAVE

↓

→ **NO** CAN'T AFFORD IT →

Food/Water
- use coupons
- buy on sale
- cut back on expensive food
- reduce trips to restaurants
- reduce spending on beverages

↓

Utilities
- turn off water when not in use
- turn off lights, reduce heat/air conditioning
- fix drafts, drips and leaks
- don't waste water, electricity, and gas

→

You're on your way to **GETTING THERE**

↑

Shelter/Security
- reduce rent · move/downsize if buying a house is not an option
- reduce the mortgage interest rate
- have lender explain what makes up a monthly payment, i.e. principal, interest, taxes, etc.
- get rid of mortgage insurance fee
- don't buy more than you can afford

"DO" RENAME OR ADD BOXES AS YOU SEE FIT

↓

Reduce and/or get rid of it!

↓

CABLE

↓

EXPENSIVE CAR

↓

BIG HOUSE

↓

SUBSCRIPTIONS

↓

GO BACK TO DO YOU NEED IT?

ABOUT THE AUTHOR

S tan Smith was born and raised in North Philadelphia, Pennsylvania. He started his career journey early at the age of seventeen by enlisting in the US Air Force. He served until he retired and went on to continue his career in IT Communications at the Veterans Administration. He holds A.A degrees in Communication/Criminal Justice from the College of the Air Force. B.A. degrees in Sociology/Criminal Justice, from University of Central Oklahoma, an MBA, MBA/Information Systems from Oklahoma City University. He is the owner of multiple residential and commercial properties and has multiple investments in stocks, bonds, and owner-operated businesses.

FORM: OUTFLOWS

OUT) Mortgage Payment (MP)	$_____MP
(OUT) Phone (PH)	$_____PH
(OUT) Car Payment (CP)	$_____CP
(OUT) Internet Service Provider (ISP)	$_____ISP
(OUT) Credit Cards (CCP) Payment	$_____CCP
(OUT) Coffee (C)	$_____C
(OUT) Eating Out (Partying) (EO)	$_____EO
(OUT) Lunch (L)	$_____L
(OUT) Water Bill (WB)	$_____WB
(OUT) Staples (Food) (S)	$_____S
(OUT) Cable TV (CTV)	$_____CTV
(OUT) Shopping for Clothing (SC)	$_____SC
(OUT) Gas (Vehicle) (GAS)	$_____GAS
(OUT) List item name	$_____
(OUT) List item name	$_____
(OUT) List item name	$_____
TOTAL: Outflows =	$_____

FORM: INFLOWS

(IN) Paycheck (PCK) (Take home) $_____month

(IN) Side Hustle Business (SHB) $_____month

(IN) Part-Time Job (PTJ) $_____month

(IN) Investments/Dividends paid out to you (IDP) $_____ month

(IN) List item name $_____

(IN) List item name $_____

(IN) List item name $_____

(IN) List item name $_____

(IN) List item name $_____

(IN) List item name $_____

(IN) List item name $_____

(IN) List item name $_____

(IN) – Total Income = $_____

WORKSHEET: CASH FLOW

Monthly Outflows (MOF) = $_____

Monthly Inflows (MIF) = $_____

MIF – MOF = $_____

Monthly Cash Flow Total (MCFT) = $_____

WORKSHEET: NET WORTH:
Asset debt owed (D)

(D) Mortgage Loan (MLND) $_____

(D) Car Loan (CLND) $_____

(D) All Credit Card Accounts (ACCND) $_____

(D) (list name of other debt) $_____

(D) (list name of other debt) $_____

(D) (list name of other debt) $_____

Total Assets Debt = $_____

WORKSHEET: NET WORTH ASSETS

LISTED NET WORTH ASSETS – Listed as (+A)

(+A) Investments (INV) (net worth) $_____

(+A) House Market Value (HMVN) (net worth) $_____

(+A) Car Value (CV) (net worth) $_____

(+A) Retirement Accounts Value (RAV) (net worth) $_____

(+A) (List name of other asset) $_____

(+A) (List name of other asset) $_____

(+A) (List name of other asset) $_____

(+A) (List name of other asset) $_____

(+A) – Total Value of Assets Owned = $_____

WORKSHEET: CALCULATE YOUR NET WORTH

Your net worth (NW$) is calculated by subtracting your debts (what you owe) (D$) from your assets (what you own) (A$). In other words, A$ – D$ = NW$.

Debt (D)   –$_____

Assets (+A)   +$_____

Net worth (NW) = A$ – D$ =$_____

STEPS TO GET YOURSELF READY TO TAKE ON YOUR GETTING THERE JOURNEY.

TO DO LIST

1. WAKE UP!
2. IF YOU HAVEN'T COMPLETELY FINISHED READING THIS BOOK, DO SO.
3. MAKE YOURSELF DO WHAT'S INSTRUCTED IN THIS BOOK.
4. ADD GETTING THERE DO'S AND SECRETS TO YOUR DAILY LIFE.
5. GET YOUR FREE CREDIT REPORTS.
6. GET YOUR FREE FINANCIAL/RETIREMENT ASSESSMENT.
7. MAKE THE TIME TO COMPLETELY UNDERSTAND AND COMPLETE THE WORKSHEETS.

   a. Inflows
   b. Outflows
   c. Other

8. SPEAK OUT LOUD THE PLEDGE ATTACHMENT.
9. SIGN YOUR PLEDGE.
10. READ THE EXERCISE AND THEN DO IT FOR YOURSELF.
11. READ THE "WORKING EXERCISE ON CUTTING WASTE" ON NEEDS AND WANTS ON (PAGE 61). GO BACK AND UNDERSTAND IT AND REVIEW THE NEEDS CHART

12. COMPLETE AN ESTATE PLAN - MINIMUM A WILL AND PUT INTO WRITING THE INSTRUCTIONS YOU WANT OTHERS TO FOLLOW.

13. HELP SOMEONE AND PURCHASE A COPY OF THIS BOOK FOR THEM.

14. MOST IMPORTANTLY AND NO MATTER WHAT, START TO INVEST.